"…one of the most readable business manuals that there is dynamite buried in every page. BOOM!"
Edwin Booth, chairman, Booth's supermarkets – from the

"Enthusiastic, passionate, encouraging and practical, based on Emma's own real-life experience – like having your own business mentor in a book."
Mike Southon, *Financial Times* columnist and co-author of *The Beermat Entrepreneur* and other business books

"Emma Wimhurst really knows what it takes to make your business BOOM! She's been there and done it and has now written the book! The only business book you will ever need!"
Jonathan Jay, entrepreneur and founder of Success Track

"Emma is a businesswoman who has delivered results and her approach to delivering results is do-able and worth reading about. She's direct and she is an entrepreneur who you can relate to. Every business owner will benefit from reading her book!"
Saira Khan, TV business presenter and founder of Miamoo Ltd

"I am delighted that Emma has written *BOOM!* I admire Emma enormously for her business acumen and go-getter approach to life and work. When Emma told me she was going to write a book to share her seven essential disciplines to positively impact a business I had no doubt that she would do it; and having read it, I now have no doubt that it will go on to be a bestseller. Emma is a highly sought after speaker who educates, engages and captivates audiences and I believe this book will do the same. The name and style of the book sums Emma up perfectly, she is dynamic, inspiring and full of passion and energy – BOOM!"
Bev James, managing director, The Coaching Academy

"Clear, honest, practical and fun, *BOOM!* is the book to get your business back on track and into the fast lane."
Faith Eckersall, columnist and lifestyle writer

"Go beyond the *BOOM!* mantra and Emma Wimhurst, like all good communicators, has a neat line in making the fundamentals of business simple. To an extent they are [simple] and should be, but all too often it's a failure to adhere to the basic disciplines that is responsible for companies foundering. By spelling it out and sharing some of her hard-earned lessons this entrepreneur hopes to save a few others and help them succeed."

Ian Wallis, editorial director and head, Entrepreneur TV

"Loaded with powerful tips, this is a book that will make you think and think again. Building on vast experience, Emma writes with sincerity in a most powerful and inspirational way."

Gill Bevis, editor, *The Business* magazine

"Emma Wimhurst is the definitive 'mumpreneur'; an ordinary mother who has allied shrewdness to energy and enthusiasm to achieve extraordinary business successes. Now Ms Wimhurst is sharing this expertise through her book, *BOOM!* Those with entrepreneurial pretensions could not wish for a better business mentor."

Sean Ashcroft, former editor, *Ambition ... Be Successful* magazine

"Emma Wimhurst has been there, done it and made a success of it so she is qualified to write about it. Her business strategies and know-how are presented with the dynamism and clarity that has become her trademark. A 'must read' for all would-be entrepreneurs."

Peter Middleton, chief executive, success.tv

"This book is brimming with passion and love. Passion for the world of the entrepreneur. That might make it sound as if *BOOM!* is a romantic novel, however it is also full of practical advice and the step by step plans of how to move your business or the business that you are planning, into the big league. Every page is laced with the understanding of someone who has been there and done it. This is a handbook for a business person, not a dry and dusty tome that will end up on the shelf unread, but one that will be referred to on a daily basis, giving you the tools to make the right decisions.

Straightforward, understandable and full of the practical tools for improving your business. I thoroughly recommend it for injecting into the entrepreneurial world the essential but often lacking ingredient of passion."

Paul Lavers, TV presenter/producer and media trainer

"Business books come and go but few can claim to make a lasting impression on their readers. *BOOM!* is not only a practical hands-on manual to help you formulate a world-beating business plan; it's also a companion that will support you throughout every stage of your business development.

The 7 Business Disciplines for success are concise and insightful, enabling you to not only place your new business on firm foundations, but also ensure you have the right skills and above all the right attitude for the trials you will face as your new business takes off.

BOOM! is certainly motivational, and also packed with practical guidance. If you're thinking of becoming an entrepreneur and stepping into the world of self-employment, read *BOOM!* first as it will equip [you] with the skills and outlook you'll need to succeed."

Dave Howell, writer, journalist and publisher, Nexus

"Emma presents some really easy to apply tips and techniques for you to apply to your business. Her no nonsense, straightforward approach makes it easy to follow. Most entrepreneurs don't realise the importance of a business plan until they have one (me included!)."

Jo Cameron, founder, Women On Their Way Ltd; media commentator and professional speaker

Emma Wimhurst is a successful entrepreneur, business owner, motivational business speaker, business mentor, broadcaster, and regular media contributor. She is founder of www.EMpwr.co.uk mentoring consultancy. Her unique, personal and highly driven mentoring style has transformed a broad range of businesses in every industry sector across the UK and overseas.

Emma speaks regularly to groups of entrepreneurs and is a frequent guest at business conferences and start-up shows. As a business expert, Emma featured on *Beat The Boss* presented by Saira Khan for BBC TV.

Emma writes regularly for *Start Your Business, Customer Strategy, The Business,* www.cmypitch.com and others and her story has been featured widely in the national press. *BOOM! 7 disciplines to CONTROL, GROW and add IMPACT to your business* is her first book. Other projects in development include a number of web-based entrepreneur projects, TV and radio.

For the latest information visit her website at:

www.emmawimhurst.com

BOOM!

7 disciplines to
CONTROL, GROW & ADD IMPACT
to your business

Emma Wimhurst
The High-Energy Business Mentor

with Sarah Sutton

Diva
publishing

First published in Great Britain in 2009 by
Diva Publishing Ltd
Fryern House, 125 Winchester Road, Chandlers Ford, Hants SO53 2DL

ISBN: 978-0-9563356-0-9

British Library Cataloguing in Publication Data
A CIP catalogue record for this book can be obtained from the British Library

Library of Congress Cataloging-in-Publication Data
A catalog record for this book is available from the Library of Congress

10 9 8 7 6 5 4 3 2 1

Text design and illustrations: Annette Peppis
Photography: Anthony Wood
Cover design and logo: Deshok.com

Printed and bound in China by WKT Co. Ltd

www.emmawimhurst.com

To my children
William, Charlie and Hattie
the BOOM!preneurs of the future

Contents

PART 2: THE BOOM! SOLUTION
7 BUSINESS DISCIPLINES FOR SUCCESS 47

PART 3: THE BOOM! BUSINESS TOOLBOX
9 PRINCIPLES OF PLANNING 161

Foreword

The first time that I met Emma was like experiencing a bracing on-shore breeze, listening to Handel's 'Arrival of the Queen of Sheba' and gulping Champagne all at the same time! There followed a flurry of enthusiasm for the task in hand, which was to be part of a team on the CBBC's 'Beat the Boss' programme. This woman rocks!

Over many years, I have met a number of people who have expressed the wish to run their own business. I have asked them why and in the majority of cases they have told me that they are fed up with working for somebody else. 'I want to control my own destiny', they say and indeed that is exactly what you do when you cast off and set sail towards the horizon on a new business venture. Woe betide, however, the business that becomes self-serving and centred on the lifestyle whims of the owner.

What comes through so clearly from Emma's advice is the need to focus on a unique idea and deliver it in such a way to impress that crucial stakeholder, the customer. Put simply, Emma encourages the reader to take an original idea and then manage it to profitable effect. On the surface this might seem quite straightforward but in reality there are many entrepreneurs who have a brilliant idea but lack the organisational and personal skills with which to take it to the market. *BOOM!* is an inspirational tool-kit for aspiring entrepreneurs and for businessmen and women who may have become becalmed and yet still have latent talents waiting to be released. Emma's tenets, and there are seven, appear regularly but are presented in a practical context and with a wealth of personal experience. This brings *BOOM!* alive and this must be one of the most readable business manuals that I have ever encountered.

Over the next 208 pages, Emma Wimhurst bares her soul and acknowledges that no business person is perfect. It is striving to succeed, however, that sets the successful business owner or manager apart. Emma will teach you that tomorrow is another day and that we are all capable of doing what we did yesterday better tomorrow. In telling the story of her business, Diva, she admits that she did not know it all but was not so proud that she would not ask for advice from her professional advisors and other businesses. Here she shares a lot in common with founders of some of the world's greatest enterprises.

So here it is, pimples and all: a business manual buzzing with acumen and based on hard experience. Emma herself will tell you that she does not have all the right answers and herein lies the infectious appeal of this book. She poses all the difficult questions and encourages us, the readers, to be honest with ourselves and attend to both our weaknesses and areas of untapped potential. So whether you are a 'starter' or a seasoned campaigner like me, there is dynamite buried in every page. BOOM!

EDWIN BOOTH, CHAIRMAN, BOOTH'S SUPERMARKETS, AUGUST 2009

PUT A BOOM!
IN YOUR
BUSINESS

Welcome to **BOOM!** the **B**usiness **O**wners' **O**perations **M**anual! written to help business owners to **B**uild, **O**wn, **O**perate, and **M**aintain their business from planning to profit.

My name is Emma Wimhurst. As a business mentor and successful entrepreneur, I believe that every business owner has tremendous untapped potential and the ability to make their business a BOOM!ing success. With increased focus, a healthy dash of self-discipline, excellent organisation and the drive to succeed, outstanding results are always possible.

I have written this book for those like me, and the people I mentor – who have already begun their business venture; those who understand the basic nuts and bolts of what is required, and are ready to take their business to the next level. They are BOOM!preneurs – entrepreneurs with the 'wow' factor, who will always go the extra mile to deliver the best possible result.

Whatever point you have reached on your business journey, my mission is to encourage and support business owners to re-focus their goals, know their true priorities and optimise profit and market potential.

Why 'BOOM!'?

A business succeeds when passion, energy, preparation and opportunity meet – and never before have so many opportunities for entrepreneurial success been open to so many people. In spite of economic challenges and world change, we are entering an exciting time of commercial potential.

Wake up your business with a ***BOOM!***

A BOOM! always makes an impact. A boom represents growth, prosperity, a loud sound or secure support. Your business BOOM! will be whatever kind of impact your business needs, to wake up, shake up or face up to changes you need to make; to regain your passion for your work and your control over your company, as you plan for growth and profit.

As you turn the pages of *BOOM!* I will introduce practical ideas that will help you to gain new perspective: showing how small changes can reap great rewards; and how large changes can propel you as far as your ambition will take you. I use real situations to demonstrate the points I am making and show you how you can use the lessons to avoid the pitfalls.

BOOM!preneurs are entrepreneurs with the 'wow' factor.

Baby BOOM!er

Being in business is in my blood. I come from a long line of Wimhursts who have always worked for themselves. I am sure that my business DNA has contributed strongly to who I am.

There are five key personality traits that are common to all entrepreneurs:

- Obsessive optimism
- Enjoyment of responsibility
- The desire to achieve
- The reward of hard work
- The urge to be entrepreneurial from childhood

These characteristics rang true for me from childhood and I also recognise them in other successful entrepreneurs. In part two of BOOM! I introduce you to 7 Business Disciplines that will help you to optimise your natural business talent – whether or not you share all the entrepreneurial traits.

According to family folklore my own business instincts first showed potential when I was about 4½ years old. My mother had settled me in the garden to play, and I disappeared. It was the milkman who spotted me first. I was out in the street, selling chocolate. My mother found me sitting on the pavement, oblivious to the anxiety I had caused her, smiling at everyone who passed – and taking cash for my wares!

Apparently I had been given a chocolate machine for my birthday, which was my pride and joy. I had somehow discovered that I could buy chocolates for 18 pence to fill my machine, but could then sell them for 24 pence – and make a 6 pence profit. I preferred selling to the older people, 'because they give me back the chocolates as well!' An early lesson learned, on knowing your target market. If only all business models were that easy!

Some thirty years later, I set up my first limited company called Diva Cosmetics. I focused solely on developing 'own-brand' colour cosmetics for non-traditional cosmetics outlets. My customers were major high street chains in the UK such as New Look, Wallis, Claire's Accessories, Mothercare, Monsoon's Accessorize, British Home Stores (BHS) and George at Asda. The company turnover grew from a very healthy £1 million in our first year of trading to several million in year four. My team grew in size from one to twelve people. The commercial margins were very healthy and within four years I was able to sell the business at a substantial profit.

The lessons I learned during that time are common to many small businesses. The purpose of this book is to reframe my experiences in a way that will help others to learn from my successes as well as my mistakes. I am now on a personal quest to help other businesses succeed. The 7 Business Disciplines that I applied rigorously to my own business are offered here with just one aim in mind – to help you and your company achieve success.

Each of us is different, with a different definition of success. Some people will want to grow and sell their business, others will want to create a legacy for their children; others are motivated more by the reward of the work itself. Most people want to spend more time with their loved ones without compromising career progression. One person's ideal life is another's worst nightmare. The truth is that you'll never find what you really want until you are happy with who you are.

Empowering your business

A few years ago I decided that the time had come to do something to help business owners to get better control over their business planning. The result is my mentoring and training company: EMpwr. EMpwr offers business mentoring and workshops to companies and individuals – as well as public speaking and media appearances. The concept stemmed from my desire to inspire and empower people in business; to help them to knock down the walls that are preventing them from achieving their full potential and to set down new foundations to secure a profitable future. My approach is firmly rooted in commercial principles, and my advice is based on personal experience.

I want to inspire people to 'have a go' – realise their dreams and fulfil their true potential.

My goal is to put the passion and idealism back into business, to inspire people from all walks of life to follow their dreams and 'have a go' – but to ground their dreams in tried and tested Business Disciplines that will support them in tough times and propel them forwards all the faster in times of growth.

At the heart of the book is my alter-ego EM. She is your small business superhero and business avatar – who will highlight the practical tips and actions. Enjoy the journey – and EM and I will be with you all the way.

Your high-energy business mentor

and **EM**
Your small business super hero

Introducing EM:
The small business
superhero

She will **empower** you to business success

EM's rule: plan for winning results

'EM' is my alter-ego. She has all the characteristics of an indestructible business superhero. EM's function in this book is simple – she is used to focus your thinking on the summary points and reminds you why the 7 Business Disciplines are so important to your success.

Wherever you see EM, you are being given a business 'takeaway' – an idea that is designed to turn your thinking from negative to positive, from 'can't do' to 'can do' – to focus your thinking, super-charge your ambitions and keep you on track.

HOW TO USE BOOM!

THE BUSINESS OWNERS' OPERATIONS MANUAL

When people come to me for mentoring they know they need to make changes, but they need some help in focusing and planning their way ahead.

- They may be *excited* by their business plans and want to BOOM! ahead.
- They may be feeling *out of control* and seeking practical tools to bring structure and discipline into their working day.
- They may have *lost focus* and with it their sense of purpose.

Sounds familiar? If so, I want to inspire you and give you the tools you need to get your business BOOM!ing – to take you as far as you want to go.

Part 1: The BOOM! mindset

Use part one to look at the mental attributes that you need to succeed. Focus on your own passion and ambition – figure out what is driving you; ask hard questions of yourself and your business and commit to planning ahead for excellent results. The Diva story includes my own business lessons as learning points and cautionary tales.

Part 2: The BOOM! solution

Use part two to understand the 7 Business Disciplines that are fundamental to the success of any business. These are not a quick fix. They are new business habits that you would be wise to instil into your business planning.

Part 3: The BOOM! business toolbox

Use part three to apply the 9 Principles of Planning to create a Business Plan. A comprehensive Business Plan is an essential tool for controlling and growing your business.

Not every company will need all seven of the business disciplines all of the time, but together they offer a plan of action that will drive positive change and profitable results. Each

The devil is in the detail.

discipline is designed to help you to control, grow and add impact to your business.

The more rigorous and detailed you can be in your planning and the more thorough your management system, the freer you will be to drive your business forward in a proactive way. The worked examples and financial models are kept deliberately simple to demonstrate the principles and lessons learned.

Four hard skills

These are the practical disciplines that affect the systems and processes that you implement within your company:

1 **Business strategy** – Focus your vision
2 **Business planning** – Build your business
3 **Marketing management** – Master your marketing
4 **Practical finance** – Manage your money

Three soft skills

These are the leadership disciplines that reflect your personal values and influence your management style in the daily running your company:

5 **Team building** – Inspire and lead your team
6 **Customer commitment** – Care for customers
7 **Personal development** – Motivate yourself

The techniques and practices are all down-to-earth, practical and straight-talking. If you are willing to apply the self-discipline, I will help you to think, plan and act like a BOOM!preneur.

The word DISCIPLINE has been chosen for a reason. It is a tough, challenging word that is designed to put you back in control. My disciplines are not rules … we all know that rules are for rebelling against and are made to be broken. They certainly are guidelines, and they are also firmly held principles – but principles are optional and guidelines are flexible – they will let you off the hook on a bad day. Disciplines on the other hand become fixed in routine, they impact on who you are, and become a practical habit. Disciplines will help you to stay on track when the going gets tough. They become an intrinsic part of the way you think, the way you act, the way you lead and the way you conduct your business.

When you apply self-discipline to your management style and business disciplines to your management structure, you can't help but improve your company's profitability and performance.

BOOM! BUSINESS BYTES

In order to succeed, in business as in life, you need to have a plan of action: to know where you are going and how you are going to get there. Planning takes organisation and sometimes a large dose of self-discipline to get it right – but the benefits are enormous and can give your business a BOOM!ing advantage that will put you ahead of your competitors.

The 7 Business Disciplines in part two will offer you practical techniques to keep your business on track to success. They will show you how to take the positive action required to become a business BOOM!preneur:

- **FOCUS your vision**
  – with business strategy
- **BUILD your business**
  – with business planning
- **MASTER your marketing**
  – with marketing management
- **MANAGE your money**
  – with practical finance
- **INSPIRE and lead your team**
  – by team building
- **CARE for customers**
  – through customer commitment
- **MOTIVATE yourself**
  – through personal development

BOOM! will help you to develop the self-discipline and planning skills that you need to succeed in business.

If you can turn the 7 Business Disciplines into practical strategies and personal habits you will be well on your way to giving your business the BOOM! factor and achieving ongoing success.

PART ONE

THE BOOM! MINDSET

How to think like a BOOM!preneur

CHAPTER 1

THE TRAITS OF A BOOM!PRENEUR

'Who wants to be an entrepreneur? – I do!' It's the cry of more and more people seduced by the desire to escape the corporate fold, who are confident that they can follow in the footsteps of self-made business dragons. Entrepreneurship is a growing 'trend'. But there is more to being a successful entrepreneur than being self-employed as anyone who has ever tried to build a business will know only too well.

Let's be quite upfront here. Running a business is not for the fainthearted. My own business story follows in the next chapter – and the path to success was not without its challenges. Motives that set you off on your own business journey – the vision of success and the excitement of your Big Idea – have to be underpinned by some rock-solid talent for business planning, the rigour of self-discipline and reliability, and the tenacity of a Rottweiler to keep you on track when the going gets tough.

Business owners who read this book will know that successful entrepreneurs are by nature proactive rather than reactive, they take the lead rather than following the pack; they seek new opportunities and love to make things happen. Making a profit is the goal – but the money alone is rarely the motive for growing a business. A passion for the project in hand, a love of the industry, enjoyment in the development process, a talent for negotiation – all of these play a part in the business choices that are made.

The heart of the matter

At the heart of every successful outcome is a cluster of personal traits that put the BOOM! in BOOM!preneurship:

■ **Absolute passion** – for life, work, people, products, for planning ahead and goal-setting, and for getting the best possible results. Driven enthusiasm lies at the heart of your motivation to be in business. Passion and leadership are natural partners. Others follow where passion leads.

■ **A 'can do' attitude** – positive in approach, full of self-belief, realistic in appraisal, brave in taking action. You will see and seek opportunities for success more readily than other people.

■ **Total honesty** – with yourself, with others, and with the ability to see the reality of every situation. You will know your weaknesses as well as your strengths and will recognise when you need to ask for help.

Rather like a three-legged stool, these three qualities work together and support one another. Take one away and the other qualities will start to lose their strength and stability.

PASSION + ATTITUDE + HONESTY = SUCCESSFUL BOOM!PRENEURSHIP

You can run a business without these traits, you can have some entrepreneurial success too; but if you are passionate in approach, can maintain a 'can do' attitude no matter what the circumstance; and have the capacity to see the absolute truth in matters, then you are more likely to have the drive and ambition required to be exceptionally successful ... **You have what it takes to be a BOOM!preneur.**

The passion factor

Passion goes hand in hand with energy. One fuels the other. Together they are the business motivators that if focused, with a clear purpose, can deliver exceptional results. Why do you need passion in business? It is the driving force that pushes you to go the extra mile – for your customers, for your team – to work hard to get things 'right'. When it is directed in a positive way, it becomes an alchemic force that can turn a group of individuals into a focused team and transform a vague idea into something of brilliance.

Passion and attitude mark the difference between excellence and mediocrity.

It is easy to spot a business or a product that has been created by people who have a passion for what they do. It is different, it has an 'edge', it raises the bar for the competition; and it is excellent, either in quality or delivery. Think Virgin, think Apple, think Dyson, think Ferrari. They are brands with the 'wow' factor. People with a passion for business are exciting to be around, they bring people together and they can be a force for change. Though, in truth, they can also be difficult to work for, changeable and exhausting in their desire to get things 'perfect'.

Keep the passion alive

Psychologists describe two kinds of motivation: *internal motivation* – which is your innate desire to do something for the sheer enjoyment of the task and *external motivation* – which is driven by the promise of a reward such as money or status. I believe that you can only feel passionate about what you do if the internal and external motivators are balanced.

Challenge yourself. Believe in what you do – because if you lose your joy in the work you'll lose your way.

This is all very well you may think, but if you haven't got it, how can you get it? If you have misplaced it, how can you get it back?

My experience as a business mentor has shown me that people tend to lose their drive when they lose their sense of purpose; when they are not getting the results they envisioned; when company growth has stalled or gone backwards.

Business passion needs to be directed towards a point of focus in order to deliver. Effective organisation, clear objectives and measured outcomes will result in:

22

- **Belief** – in yourself, your product, your purpose and your potential.
- **Validation** – from the market, from mentors, from your colleagues.
- **Results** – driven by planning ahead, setting goals, hard work and monitoring results.

The attitude audit

Once the buzz and the excitement of doing business are in your blood there is, as far as I know, no cure. It is a type of madness in some ways that involves taking risks, using intuition, facing fears, seeing viable opportunities where others see lost causes and taking a leap of faith into the unknown.

Your personal attitude when under pressure will tell you whether you are a 'can do' or a 'can't do' kind of person and the impact you have on those around you. The difference between the two can mean the difference between success and failure in business. The good news is that your attitude can change. If you want to be a 'can do' person, you can. There is no room for negativity in the mind of the BOOM!preneur.

Make money your motivator

Your attitude to money is also important and is closely aligned to your likelihood of success. When you are responsible for paying yourself, it really *does* matter if there are no sales today/ this week/month; it really *does* matter if a marketing campaign is not delivering revenue and has been a waste of money; it really *does* matter if you have a member of staff who is consistently late or makes mistakes; it really *does* matter if goods are less than perfect. It's one thing to have faith and self-belief, it is quite another to sail through thinking that 'something' will turn up.

Think 'Can do' and banish the 'Can'ts'.

Ultimately there are very few businesses that don't need to make money. Managing your finances is important. You are not running a hobby, you are running a business. If you are not 'on the money' and you're consistently out of cash, you need to take steps fast to turn things around. It really is your top priority.

Love what you do

Many problems in business stem from a lack of self-belief that translates to customers as a lack of interest in their requirements. There is no place in business for anyone who is not 100 per cent committed or does not have total belief in the quality and efficacy of their business service. Why would anyone buy from a retailer who apologises for his stock selection? No advert would succeed if the sales message contained a caveat to say, 'We know it's not brilliant but we hope it will do.' A money-back guarantee is meant as a guarantee of success, not a get-out clause. A lack of enthusiasm, a lack of interest, or the appearance of being purely profit-oriented will send potential customers into the arms of the competition.

A positive attitude is what wins business at the end of the day.

Customers like consistency, they believe in brand loyalty. When you are running a business your brand is *you*, and your customer wants to 'buy' what you represent. As part of the business exchange you owe it to them as well as to yourself to make sure that your brand values are consistent, reliable and deliver on your promise.

Keep on learning

Having a mind that is closed is dangerous in business. Business is all about learning – because markets change, technology changes and customers' needs change. When change comes you need to be ahead of the curve. 'Adapt or die' as Darwin so memorably put it – or 'adapt and learn', which is my preferred approach.

24

If you don't know something – take advice. It's a better use of your time and will deliver results more quickly.

You may be an expert in your profession, with years of business experience – but that doesn't mean you have all the skills you need to succeed. Keep an open mind and ask questions – it will help you to overcome problems more effectively. Being totally self-reliant can leave you at a disadvantage. Much better to track down several experts and keep asking 'What?' and 'Why?' and 'How?' to broaden your choices.

Time spent finding out what is going on at grassroots level in your industry can also keep you feeling positive and in control. It's important to stay in tune with what is going on technologically as well as economically; it may impact on how you spend your plant costs, re-skill yourself or your workforce, or how you source your suppliers.

Welcome the challenges

As an entrepreneur you need to be good at finding solutions – because you will be faced with many brick walls on your business journey and may even crash into a few of them. Everybody does. Nobody is without problems. What will differentiate you from your competitors is what you do about the obstacle. Do you knock it down, go around it, find a way over it? Or do you avoid it, justify it, procrastinate or deny it? It is your response in times of trouble that will make you successful.

Entrepreneurs need to enjoy the process of problem-solving.

The power of honesty

The third core trait of a BOOM!preneur is honesty – being honest with yourself and those around you. We all kid ourselves sometimes and it is the toughest trait to master in many ways. It is about being assertive, speaking up, speaking out and speaking

Honesty is what gives passion a clear point of focus and attitude its energy.

bravely, even when you would rather not have to; acknowledging when *you* are at fault, and always taking responsibility for your thoughts and actions.

Honesty has little to do with self-deprecation, making excuses, or always taking the blame yourself – those are negative habits that have no place in business. It means showing people exactly who you are and not what you think they want to see. It frees up your brain to develop clarity of focus. Honesty helps you to see exactly what you want and direct every atom of your being towards achieving it. It also requires thought and consideration. Honesty is not an excuse for blunt talking or rudeness. Respect is an essential part of effective business dealings.

Pause for thought

Not everyone will choose to have a business mentor, but everyone in business needs to re-evaluate their goals and to review their financial results on a regular basis. The review should include self-assessment too. Re-focusing on your end goal and your current priorities will enable you to adjust your position and keep on track.

REVIEW ▶ PLAN ▶ DO ▶ REVIEW

Following is a summary of the kinds of questions that may be covered during a series of mentoring sessions. They reveal a lot about the 'why's and 'how's of business planning and personal motivation. A period of review can be useful in re-assessing a situation or adjusting a plan of action. Pausing for thought will help you to see the wood for the trees in your business.

26

Review your position:

- Why am I doing this?
- What is it I really want?
- Where is my business heading and am I happy about its direction?
- Do I still get enjoyment from my work? And if not, why not?
- How do I want to develop my business, and what is stopping me forging ahead?
- Do I want to sell the business, or do I want to leave a family legacy?
- What do I want to have achieved in five or ten years time?

Plan ahead

- What is the one most important thing that would improve the situation right now?
- What steps do I need to take to achieve my main objective?
- What additional skills and knowledge do I need to bring about the necessary change?
- What level of investment do I need?
- What time frame can I achieve it in?

Take action

- What are my start and end dates?
- What actions should I schedule?
- How will I project manage and monitor progress?
- Who do I need to help me to achieve my goals?
- When can I start?

Review again, and repeat.

There are no wrong and no right answers – there are only those answers that will lead you to plan for an outcome that is right for your business. Remember – as a business owner you are *always* the master of your own destiny!

Take a long-term view

As in the story of the tortoise and the hare, it is the well-organised business owners who direct their passion with strategic savvy and well-paced stamina that deliver the lasting results. Most young entrepreneurs of course are more like hares in their approach, desperate to get things moving and to get ahead of the competition. That style of approach may work in the start-up phase of business development but won't support you through the long haul of strategic growth.

With a few years' experience under their belts most business owners come to realise that you don't need to be the company that heads the pack to be the most profitable, and you will gain far greater respect for consistently achieving what you set out to do rather than burning out, selling out or going bankrupt. Business is not a sprint, it is a marathon: a way of life, a way of thinking and a way of being.

It is true that there is no such thing as an overnight success and nor do you grow a company that makes £1 million turnover without taking a few risks and making some big decisions along the way. The eventual success may be perceived as luck by those looking in from the outside but is rarely a surprise to the mind behind the plan. The following chapter takes a closer look at the business lessons that influence business decision-making.

Being successful in business requires patience as well as timing.

BOOM! BUSINESS BYTES

Many people have the desire to run their own business and many have the commercial know-how, the technical skill or the industry knowledge to enable them to succeed.

Your entrepreneurial nature will make you the master of your own business destiny.

However, not everyone is cut out to be a business-owner, no matter how entrepreneurial their instincts. Those who find it hard to sell their skills, who find personal organisation a challenge or, worse, are poor money managers, should make sure they are well supported by professionals with complementary skills before they begin.

BOOM!preneurs are entrepreneurs with the 'wow' factor. They have commercial abilities and drive aplenty; they know their strengths and weaknesses – and they have a laser-sharp fix on their personal goals. They also have the passion, the positive attitude and the capacity for personal honesty that enables them to go the extra mile – to be the best they can be. Have you got the character traits of a BOOM!preneur? Are you:

- **Goal** orientated
- **Opportunity** seeker
- Aware of own **strengths** and **weaknesses**
- Always wants to **be the best**
- **Enjoys** work
- **Seeks help** when required
- Has **passion, attitude, honesty**
  … and the **drive** to succeed

As a business owner you are the master of your own destiny – you can choose to develop the 'can do' attitude that will give you the BOOM! factor and plan ahead to ensure you will succeed.

CHAPTER 2

BIG DECISIONS AND BOOM!ING SUCCESSES

(AND BUSINESS LESSONS ALONG THE WAY)

There will always be business mavericks; those whose decisions appear to be so impetuous that their new ventures seem nothing short of a wild gamble. Charisma and passion are common characteristics amongst risk takers – in every field. However, look more closely and you will usually find that those who succeed are only ever impetuous on the surface.

Somewhere in the mix of every successful entrepreneurial venture you will find an astute business brain at work with a talent for decision-making; a willingness to delegate; and exceptional knowledge or passion for their product or industry. Impulsiveness is often compensated for by other factors: backing from family or corporate investors perhaps; involvement of industry experts or financial advisors who add finesse to the Business Plan and temper the extremes of over-optimism; a media or business deal that underwrites some of the risk; or perhaps a 'do or die' situation where the alternative is as extreme as bankruptcy.

The business risks worth taking are the ones that can be supported by industry knowledge and thorough research that is second to none; by a commitment to financial management that would make a bank manager proud; and by a level of planning that would allow your business to keep running smoothly even if you suffered from amnesia and forgot the company was yours. You may not always plan to make a profit, but you must know why you are embarking on the venture, be ready to make hard decisions and know what its market offering will be.

Every big decision is a calculated risk

There are four main themes in this chapter, each intended to help guide your business plans:

- **The Diva story** – My experiences as the owner and managing director of a start-up company offer validation for my business recommendations, based on varied personal experience and profitable results.

- **BIG decisions** – The BIG decision moments that shaped Diva's success are used to explain the vital part played by my 7 Business Disciplines; and to encourage you to apply them to your own business future.

- **BIG risks** – These underline my personal philosophy that even though entrepreneurs and business owners must be willing to take risks to be successful – with their money, with investors' money and sometimes with their future security – those risks can be turned into *calculated* risks.

- **Thinking BIG** – I want to help every business person to see that thinking BIG takes the same amount of effort as thinking small, to encourage and help plan for the BIG decision moments in every business plan that can lead to success.

The Diva story

I always say that Diva Cosmetics was my third business. My first was my mini-chocolate enterprise; my second, set up when I was 18 years old and living in Andorra, was as an English teacher; and then ten or so years later Diva Cosmetics was born.

In the intervening years I leaned how business works from a corporate perspective, primarily while working for Revlon cosmetics in the UK. The first five years gave me solid experience at the sharp end of manufacturing and production: sourcing materials, learning how to negotiate, honing profit margins and absorbing every aspect of the production process. It wasn't the glamorous end of the cosmetics industry, but I was fascinated by the whole process. The experience gave me an extraordinary advantage when it came to setting up my own cosmetics company. I also learned my first business lesson: control your costs.

Business lesson: Keep tight control over your costs.

Restless to learn more, I joined the Revlon head office in London as a marketing assistant. I loved my job and had the opportunity to gain some valuable business insights from the senior management team. I learned from them the value of others' experience and how important it is for business leaders to share their wisdom with those who are just starting to learn.

By the time I left Revlon I had solid experience in new product development, merchandising and promotions, a valuable network of industry contacts, a solid reputation and an in-depth understanding of

Business lesson: You build business by building relationships.

the cosmetics industry. With an increasing desire to work for myself, I was raring to do something exceptional. The only thing that was holding me back from achieving my goals – was me. I didn't know how to use my knowledge and experience … yet!

Waking up to my 'big idea'

Every idea has its time, and every person knows when they are ready to take action. During much of the 1990s the mood of the country was buoyant. We had not yet become embroiled in the chaos of a world post 9/11. Princess Diana was becoming an international icon known for her glamour and beauty – and 'Girl Power' BOOM!ed into our lives as the Spice Girls became *the* pop phenomenon in the UK. They encapsulated the spirit of the time.

To anyone thinking of setting up a new venture, no matter how experienced in business, I say – *first* become an industry expert, then *plan* what you are going to do. Only then should you take action. (Remember: Review, Plan, Do, Review).

The all-girl pop group epitomised the positive mood of the nineties. Their music was uplifting and their dancing was high

34

energy. There was something unique and fresh about their style and vivacity.

I woke up to what was happening and was very interested in the enormous influence they were having – especially on young girls and teenagers. Everyone had a favourite Spice Girl and wanted to look like them. The girls wore bright colours and strong make-up that reminded me of the vibrancy of the 1970s.

My idea didn't come to me as a lightning bolt, but I did start to look closely at the teenage market. I began to ask questions: 'Where do teenagers buy fashion?' 'How much do they spend?' 'Where do they buy their colour cosmetics?'

I realised with excitement that there was a close synergy between fashion purchases and choice of make-up. My 'big idea' was the realisation that colour make-up was *a fashion driven line*. I felt strongly that there was an opportunity to produce 'own-brand' ranges of colour cosmetics that the well-known high street stores could sell under

Business lesson: Always find out where and why people buy.

their own labels. I saw the cosmetics as impulse buys that would sell alongside their fashion ranges. I was filled with enthusiasm and anticipation and couldn't wait to get started.

I began by taking a close look at the competition and thought carefully about which stores would benefit most from my idea. Two fashion chains were already selling branded make-up, but there was also a new company that had exactly the right profile for my concept: New Look. I knew the owners had ambitious plans for store development and were buying retail units across the UK. There was a real energy about the company and I had them firmly in my sights.

Business lesson: Have the courage to do things your way.

Testing the market

In those early months it was definitely the 'brilliant idea' that was driving me forwards rather than the idea of setting up a company for the sake of it. A large percentage of businesses start out with sole trader status rather than setting up straight away as a limited company. There are many advantages to this – not least the flexibility of being able to team up with other people on an associate basis. So with my savings to see me through the learning stages, I became self-employed.

I wouldn't say that I had a business strategy firmly etched at this point. It was much more about testing the market in those early months. However, I was very ambitious and I was already heading up a successful enterprise in my mind. Ever the organiser, I had sketched out a Business Plan and costings, based on my naïve assumption that the team at New Look would be so impressed by my ideas that they would immediately buy in to my entire concept. When I secured an appointment to make my pitch, I was already prepared.

Pitching for success

Never one to do anything by halves, I had put together an extensive presentation explaining how I thought a colour cosmetics line should be positioned in-store at every branch of New Look. I envisioned metre-wide bays that I could fill with every colour and type of cosmetic. But I hadn't really thought things through. The business lessons were about to arrive thick and fast.

I ventured forth and gave the buyers the presentation of my life. I paused for breath and waited for the validation that my idea had wowed them. It came, but not in the form I had expected. I hadn't planned for a 'But' …

Business lesson: Become a market expert before you meet your customers.

36

Business lesson: Never assume that you know more than the customer about what they need.

They said, 'We love your energy, we love your enthusiasm, we love everything you have shown us. BUT… *we don't want to take make-up in the way you have described*.'

To say I was devastated was an understatement. I could hardly speak. I had done so much work and my idea was being dashed to the ground before it had had a chance to fly. I tried hard to focus on what was being said. Pilferage was a particular concern from their point of view.

I felt utterly disappointed. And then I heard another 'but' … as in, '*BUT – we would like to trial nail polish.*'

People have asked me since, 'How did you feel at that point?' I felt so strongly that they ought to have taken the whole range, I was just deflated. I really couldn't see the point in them taking just the nail polish.

But it was me who didn't get the point. Clearly they understood their customers very well, but they had to test their market. From memory I think that early order was for 20,000 units, which was a fabulous result. New Look was about to launch its first own-brand nail polishes and my Big Idea was becoming reality.

I hadn't really done own-label selling before but I was quick to learn. I sourced the bottles, chose the style and design, and developed ten nail polish colours. It took about 6–7 weeks from the time I received the order to deliver the stock to their door – on a Wednesday I think.

And then the good news … five days later I got a call. Everything had sold out over the weekend and they needed to place another order – double the size.

I was exhilarated. That was the moment when I began to feel this really could lead to something exciting. I had secured my first deal and the beginning of the realisation of my dream.

Going it alone

1999 was a busy year. The Wallis clothing chain had become my second client. Although their orders were relatively small, having two brand names on board was a real advantage. However, not everything was going as smoothly as planned.

I had teamed up during this period with a business associate and friend who was very keen to work with me and valued my knowledge of the cosmetics industry. He had broader commercial experience than I did and I had been bouncing my ideas off him for some time. He was an excellent mentor to me during the early days and it was good to know he was there as I stepped out into unknown territory. I felt safer knowing that I was sharing the business risk.

The two of us enjoyed the early successes and divided the profits and I knew I couldn't have achieved what I had done without him. But with every pitch I made and every order I received, my new territory was fast making sense and looking familiar.

It's very important, as far as possible, to work with people who are a 'match' for your own energy, values and working methods. With a great sense of sadness I began to realise that as business colleagues, my friend and I were incompatible. We shared a passion for success, and a love of the industry, but our attitudes to crucial elements of the planning and delivery process were so different that we were pulling against one another in style and approach. I knew I had to have the honesty to face the situation head on and step away. I had to be free to do things my way. We parted company. It was a very, very painful lesson.

Now that I was totally on my own I realised that I needed to establish my own business and start to do things properly. I also needed an assistant: someone who had detailed knowledge and

Business lesson: Every situation has a positive side to it. It's how you deal with mistakes that makes the difference in life.

a passion for colour. Enter Nicky Connors, who was to become a mainstay of the business. She remained with me until I sold the company nearly four years later.

The birth of Diva

Diva Cosmetics Ltd was founded on 14 January 2000, almost a year to the day after the birth of my firstborn son, William. I still use the same solicitor and accountant that I had in those early days. They joined me at Diva's first strategy meeting and have been with me every step of the way since. There is a lot to be said for establishing rock solid legal and financial foundations from the very start in business.

Nicky and I moved into serviced offices in Bournemouth, Dorset. (I had been advised against committing to a long-term lease or rental at this stage.) I focused first on developing new business contacts and Claire's Accessories was about to become a new major client. Our competitors hardly noticed us at first because we

Business lesson: Don't commit to heavy overheads at start-up stage. Start small and secure the foundations first.

were operating on a reltively modest scale. We were quite happy with small orders from our own-brand customers. From there we grew steadily, and achieved a turnover of over £1 million in our first year. We had arrived!

I wanted to be the leading expert in colour cosmetics, so we needed to stay ahead of market trends. To understand what our customers might want, we had to know what was going on around the world. Nicky and I did a lot of travelling – within the UK and to trade fairs in Europe. We were managing all the business we could handle, but our order numbers were increasing at a rate that meant I needed more staff. With the help of my lawyer and my accountant, I had to start planning for growth.

Business lesson: Always plan ahead for business growth.

Gearing up for growth

Planning for growth isn't simply a matter of expanding or taking on new customers; it involves *reviewing* every area of your business – including the capacity of your third-party suppliers to deliver results – and then planning your strategy. A Business Plan is an essential tool. Use your Business Plan as a starting point for review (and if you don't have one, create one. See page 62). Take professional advice from an accountant with strategic experience. It is too high risk to take on new staff and new business without an expert to help you to assess what you can afford and when; and what you will need to do, by when, to make your growth plans work.

My aim at Diva was to grow my company from start-up to profit as soon as possible. I reviewed my Business Plan every six months, and some elements of it more frequently than that. The financial year ran from January to December and each year I would review our growth to date and assess our customer base and the workflow. Each new staff appointment was carefully planned and budgeted in line with plans for growth and expectations of the marketplace. My Business Plan was a vital anchor point that also enabled my accountant, my bank manager and my team to understand my ambitions and business capability.

Always plan ahead

Take account of any additional requirements that you will need, to ensure that you can deliver on your promises to all of your customers. Distribution networks, customer service and IT requirements or marketing materials: every work function and every detail should be considered and scrutinised to ensure consistency of approach and quality of delivery. Where is the money coming from to fund the expansion? There will usually be a proportion of outlay required before you gain financial returns. Do you need to borrow from the bank? Take advice before you do so.

40

Business lesson: Take professional advice to help you plan effectively for growth.

Your most important business asset during any kind of expansion programme is your people – new and existing. Expansion offers an opportunity to reward existing staff with promotion and an increase in responsibility. Anyone who will soon be a manager should be involved in your plans to recruit for their team.

Building the dream team

I recognised from the outset that for Diva to succeed as a company it was important to get the right team in place. I needed to recruit people who would pull together in the same direction – with a similar work ethic. In the early stages of team building it is essential to recruit people who have skills and character that complement your own; to increase understanding and reduce the likelihood of conflict. The development of corporate culture is a subtle and organic process. I knew I wanted positivity, energy and commitment in abundance, so I was very careful about who came into the Diva fold.

Few people who dream of setting up in business will look at the management function too closely in advance – unless of course a large team is needed from the outset. Most business owners envisage hiring people to deliver what they need, as and when they need them. They don't foresee the minor dramas of hiring, firing, motivating and managing people. And yet, the challenge of building a positive, happy and productive team is the greatest challenge of all.

Business lesson: Hire bright and enthusiastic people at assistant level and grow them with the business.

I talk a lot in part two about the importance of 'matching'. A small- to medium-sized company has no spare capacity to 'carry' someone who is not performing to the same standard and representing the same values as the rest of the team. Rectifying mistakes retrospectively is expensive. It is much, much better to take your time, interview rigorously and ensure that the preferred candidate has the right skills for the job and the character to match.

Setting objectives and outcomes

Always set objectives and outcomes that support your market position. As a team, our joint expertise differentiated us from any of our competitors. That's why the Diva concept worked. We never tried to sell to our clients, we approached them as experts in colour cosmetics, with the market knowledge to help them to anticipate new trends and gain better understanding of what their customers were likely to buy. My team knew that it was 'my way or the highway', which was tough but necessary, especially during the early days. They rose to the challenge and delivered great results. I was very excited about the future.

Business lesson: Turn up the heat on your business – set your outcomes before you begin.

Towards the end of 2001 I recognised that over 50 percent of our business was now with a single customer. This was not a good position to be in. I needed to get new business on board. It was with that in mind that I took the decision to invest in marketing our business.

Diva therefore invested in a website, and a lavish brochure which was extremely expensive to produce. The brochure told potential customers everything that they needed to know about Diva. It was designed to show our company values.

I needed only one new customer to break even on the investment. In fact it generated *three* new customers, over a fifteen-month period. It had been a huge gamble – but what a fantastic result. Our new clients were: River Island, George at Asda and British Home Stores.

42

The rise of Diva

The years that followed were hard work but enormous fun. We grew to become a team of twelve and travelled all over the world. One of the most crucial aspects of our success at Diva was our ability to clarify our objectives and always to position ourselves as market specialists. We had to know exactly what the latest trends were so that we could beat our competitors to market. Buying trips to Hong Kong, Los Angeles, New York and Paris sound glamorous but were essential. Further investment went into understanding what made consumers tick. What drove their buying decisions – was it the packaging, the price point, the promise? We adapted our approach to the needs of each customer but never compromised on our own company values of fairness, honesty, quality and delivering consistent results.

Business lesson: Keep asking questions, even when you think you know the answer.

Three years and ten months after I started Diva, I sold the company at a significant profit. I had been unable to share my plans with my team, so it was a huge shock to them when I made the announcement. However, I had found a buyer who had solid plans for the company and who wanted to take the business forwards – keeping my team in place. I was pleased that I had been able to secure a deal that would safeguard their jobs and their futures. The Diva years had been special and it was hard to let go. However, selling is what makes the business world work and so I stepped away happily – my children had become the greater priority at the time.

SMALL actions lead to BIG decisions that create BOOM!ing results.

THE DIVA STORY: 7 BUSINESS DISCIPLINES IN THE MAKING

■ **The Diva Vision**

Our clear vision statement gave everyone a shared sense of purpose and focus and helped me to make good decisions about the future growth and direction of the business.

(See *Business Discipline No.1: Business Strategy*, page 50)

■ **The Diva Business Plan**

I knew what I wanted to achieve and my Business Plan kept me on target for growth – not only financially but also strategically. I used it to convey a clear message to third parties and to give the business some direction and momentum.

(See *Business Discipline No.2: Business Planning*, page 62)

■ **The Diva Marketing Plan**

We created own-brand cosmetics for high street chains and quality brands. We did not sell products direct to consumers. Marketing was the one area where I took calculated risks in order to raise the profile of Diva as a company and to target and win new customers. I invested heavily to ensure we were known internationally and to showcase our product. I wanted to demonstrate our values and to show that we had exceptional industry knowledge. The strategy worked, but make no mistake – every penny of every marketing campaign was assessed for outcome vs. investment.

(See *Business Discipline No.3: Marketing Management,* page 78)

■ **Tight cost control**

A highly efficient and cashflow system and extremely tight cost control were the true reasons for Diva's commercial success.

(See *Business Discipline No.4: Practical Finance,* page 96)

44

▪ Building a team that matched

Diva grew from a team of two to a team of twelve within four years. We were an almost perfect match when it came to character and complementary in our skills. Twelve was a small enough number for me to feel I had a relationship with each member of the team and could stay in touch with what was going on – but large enough to allow for delegation and teamwork.

(See *Business Discipline No.5: Team Building*, page 116)

▪ Protecting customers' interests

Our customers were our livelihood and as such their interests had to be protected at all times. My word has always been my bond and in business there are no exceptions. That meant absorbing the cost if our shipments were delayed en route from the Far East, as happened on occasion. I made sure that our business model included a contingency for delays and could handle a few setbacks.

(See *Business Discipline No.6: Customer Commitment*, page 134)

▪ Personal time

I am a business person to the core and tend to be 'all or nothing' in my commitment. By 2003 I was also a mother, and felt pulled in conflicting directions.
I changed my focus to find a way to create better balance between my work and home life.

(See *Business Discipline No.7: Personal Development*, page 148)

PART TWO

THE BOOM! SOLUTION

7 business disciplines for success

If you plan for success, you will achieve it.

THE HARD SKILLS

I have a fundamental belief that underpins everything that I do and say – if you **plan** for success, you **will** achieve it.

My Business Disciplines 1–4 will help you to plan and achieve whatever you want and take you wherever your ambition leads you. They are the building blocks of business, without which you would be unable to survive. They are the practical disciplines that affect the systems and processes that you implement within your company.

What is the purpose of a Strategic Plan?

It is a vision statement that:

- Identifies your company's goals
- Provides a framework for making commercial decisions
- Aids with business planning
- Motivates and informs
- Is concise – no more than 50 words

BUSINESS STRATEGY

FOCUS YOUR VISION

Do you have 2020 vision? By which I mean, do you know where your business will be in one year, five years or in the year 2020? Your Strategic Plan forms your company DNA. It reminds you of your company's roots, of the reason you started your business and where you aim to be in the marketplace of the future.

Bring your business into focus

The secret of success in business is clarity – clarity of purpose, planning and direction. The first of the 7 BOOM! Business Disciplines focuses on defining your business goals and ambitions in the form of a Strategic Plan: a vision statement that encapsulates what your company does, who your customers are, what you want your business to achieve, how you are going to achieve it, and over what timescale.

I am always amazed by the number of business owners I speak to who are unable to tell me concisely what it is they do or where they are headed. A Strategic Plan is more than just a passive statement. It encapsulates your vision for your business. It is an anchor point and your touchstone for evaluating every decision that you make – from your choice of staff, to your choice of client; from your financial goals to your capital expenditure; from your expansion plans to your decision to sell the business. A company message that is congruent with what is delivered to the marketplace projects total confidence and will attract ongoing business.

Don't confuse business goals with personal goals.

Identify your company's goals

A company that doesn't know where it is going or what it is doing is in danger of losing its way. If your business has a tendency to say 'yes' to any and every business assignment that comes along, without evaluating whether it makes commercial and strategic sense to do so – then it is time to review your strategic goals.

Strategic goals should not be confused with your personal goals, even though you may work for yourself. A Strategic Plan is not about your personal achievement ('I want to earn enough money to retire by the age of 50'). A Strategic Plan is all about planning and positioning your business ('To become the premier supplier to the industry within five years').

A Strategic Plan is not rigid. It can be adapted – and it should be from time to time – to reflect changes in the marketplace and stay in line with your company's plans for growth. But deviate from the plan only if you are doing so consciously – with full awareness of the ramifications for workflow and cashflow.

Ask yourself the following questions:

- Could you sum up your business in 50 words?
- Do you know where you want your business to be in one, five or ten years?
- Do you have a vision statement to refer to when facing difficult decisions?
- Is the main focus of your business the same now as it was when you started?
- Are you headed consciously in a deliberate direction, or are you reacting only to the opportunities that drift through your door?
- Do all your stakeholders understand what your business is about and where it is going?
- How do you currently decide who to work with and what to do? Do you rely on 'gut feel'?

If the answer to any of these questions is 'no', the recommendations in this chapter will help you to refocus your goal and your plans. A gut feeling isn't enough. You need to have a plan.

A framework for decision-making

Your Strategic Plan is your framework for making commercial and value-based decisions. It will help you to say 'yes' to good decisions and to know what to avoid.

It may seem strange to suggest that a Strategic Plan is an important tool for deciding when to turn business away, but staying true to your business ethos is very important, not only in sending a consistent message to your customer base, but also to your staff and suppliers.

Time is money in business – it is a cliché but it is true. Accepting work that diverts you from your core business focus, however tempting, will usually take up more of your time than you had anticipated and may jeopardise other projects. The decision to diversify must always be taken consciously rather than reactively.

An aid to business planning

Your Strategic Plan works in partnership with Business Discipline No.2 – Business Planning. It is your route map – because you can't draw up an overview of the business without first knowing what it is you want to achieve. When you are offered a new business opportunity, stop and ask:

■ Will the new business add to or detract from the core aims of your business?
■ Will the new business reinforce the business identity that you have been presenting to your customers or does it send a confused message?
■ Will the new business add value to your business in a way

54

that will give you market advantage and put you ahead of the competition?

■ Will the new business prevent you from focusing on bringing in more of your core business?

■ How much will it cost in terms of cashflow and workflow?

■ Have you got the resources to enable it to happen?

If you can deliver results using the resources and networks that you already have in place, it is likely to be plainer sailing and more cost-effective.

If you need to invest in new resources in order to deliver, ensure you are making a wise choice for your business.

Motivate and inform

One of the purposes of a Strategic Plan is to communicate a very clear business message that will help you and your team to feel confident that there is uniformity of purpose and clear goals surrounding everything you do. Time spent on clarifying your Strategic Plan means that no matter who or what you encounter, you will be able to explain very clearly and precisely what your business is for; you and your team will think and behave more congruently; and you will be far more confident when meeting the bank, or your accountant, solicitor and clients.

Knowing your business values and clarifying the vision will impact on every one of the BOOM! Disciplines – from business expenditure to marketing and branding.

Your strategic plan in 50 words

It should always be possible to summarise your Strategic Plan in no more than 50 words – no matter how complicated the structure of the business. Any shorter and something important has been left out; any longer and your statement lacks focus.

Getting the strategy right will give you confidence: a 'feel good' awareness that, 'Yes, that works. I feel enthusiastic and upbeat when I tell people that is what we are all about.' The statement should be motivational and informative – and it should convey the same message to everybody that you encounter.

The Diva Cosmetics' Strategic Plan stated my ambition clearly:

To be the No.1 preferred supplier of own-label colour cosmetics and gift sets to fashion retailers on the high street within three years. To consistently deliver excellence in terms of customer service, quality and new product ideas, ensuring our customers are providing the best choice possible on the high street. (50 words)

Let's break that down a little.

A Strategic Plan is made up of four separate elements:

1   The proposition – What you are offering in terms of product or services.

'To be the No.1 preferred supplier of own-label colour cosmetics and gift sets …'

2   The target market – Who you are talking to and want to attract.

'… to fashion retailers on the high street …'

3   The delivery – How you are going to deliver your proposed service.

'To consistently deliver excellence in terms of customer service, quality and new product ideas'

4   The desired outcome for your client – Make sure that your benefit to them is clear.

'… ensuring our customers are providing the best choice possible on the high street.'

Focus on the goal

Take a moment to review your business goals. What are they? Do they differ from your goals when you started up the company? Write them down. Throw out any that are not true and keep only those that serve you and your business well.

Now allow yourself some time to focus solely on your strategy statement. You may have one already – in which case take time to consider whether it is working for you or whether it is time to refocus the vision. Think about where you want your business to be in ten years' time. Think of words and phrases that encapsulate the essence of what you want to achieve, where you want to be. Your statement has to be exciting and needs to motivate.

The proposition

Be clear about what you are offering in terms of product/service. Choose the words and phrases that best summarise your proposition, as in the following example:

Executive search   Professional

Market experts   Advice on hiring strategy

Specialising in the environmental sector

Retained services   Reliable, knowledgeable

Total recruitment service   Telephone screening

Your target market

Define who you are talking to i.e. your target market.

Capture on paper all the categories and type of business you are aiming at. Underline those that encapsulate your market the best – and add those to your statement.

Planning consultancies   Public sector

Construction firms   Private sector

Environmental specialists

Engineering firms   Private investors

Delivery

Identify *how* you are going to deliver your proposed product/ service outcome – ensure that the benefits are clear to potential customers.

work in partnership with clients

wide range of contacts

fast and efficient delivery

total confidentiality

58

Desired outcome

Identify, from your clients' point of view, the benefits of choosing your company.

Excellent matching   Time-saving

Good value for money

Efficient service   Competitive advantage

Now put it all together:

FUTURE PEOPLE – Environmental Recruitment Specialists

Future People is an award-winning company, specialising in executive search and selection in the environmental sector. Our highly qualified and well-connected team of industry specialists works in partnership with public and private sector clients to identify requirements, provide recruitment advice, screen CVs and submit short-list candidates for excellent results. (Total: 49 words)

Being this clear doesn't mean your plan won't change; you should review your strategy statement regularly in the light of market changes and your own vision for the future.

Once you have created a plan that is 'right', you will find that you use it frequently to communicate, both internally and externally, exactly what you are all about; and to make sure that everyone who works with you is pulling in the same direction.

Follow your strategy

My main focus during the first eighteen months of building Diva Cosmetics was to find new ways to grow the business.

Imagine how thrilled I was when we were approached by a licensing company that wanted a range of products for children and teenagers featuring Oliver Postgate's *Bagpuss* – a lovable cat character featured on a children's television series. They wanted us to create a range of gift sets and make-up. The big brand opportunity went straight to my head. I said, 'Yes of course, we'd love to do that.' My team came up with a fabulous range of ideas. We asked our suppliers in the Far East to create samples of an amazing array of products. The heart and soul of the whole team went into the preparation for our presentation.

On the surface the opportunity appeared to be a perfect match for Diva: the product was targeting the same retail outlets, the same consumers and using the same suppliers as our own-brand cosmetics *but* there were flaws in the opportunity from Diva's point of view:

It became very clear very quickly that the business model was very high risk for Diva. I would become a licensee for the brand: Diva would produce and buy the stock, hold it and then sell it on to customers. It was a totally different business model to our own-brand business. It would put severe pressure on our cashflow and would tie up capital in stock that we had no guarantee of selling. The reality made me stop and question. Did this high-profile branded assignment fit the Diva profile – and could we afford to take it on? It was an extremely important question.

Referring back to my Strategic Plan made the decision to walk away so much quicker and easier. The Diva vision was, 'to be the No.1 preferred supplier of own label colour cosmetics … on the high street' The Diva plan did *not* say, 'to become the supplier of licensed goods'.

Turning down any kind of business opportunity will always go against the entrepreneurial grain. Had I not had my Strategic Plan, and stayed true to that plan, I may very well have made a bad decision for Diva.

BOOM! BUSINESS BYTES

Developing a clear business strategy that can be summed up in 50 words or less, will help you take a proactive rather than a reactive approach to growing your business. A BOOM!ing strategy statement will keep you focused and help you to see whether or not an opportunity is a genuine match for your business. It will give other people a clear and consistent view of what your business is about.

Appearances can be deceptive. In the case of the *Bagpuss* opportunity (see opposite), the types of product we were producing fitted our business profile and the end consumers were the same as Diva's usual target market. However – the Business Plan gave me the clarity to see what was wrong:

■ **Define your core business activity** – Diva *created* product, we did *not* sell, store or distribute product. The contract would have led to a significant increase in our overheads.

■ **Don't jeopardise your profits** – Changing Diva's business model reactively and for a single product line, rather than planning a change strategically for a range of lines would not have been cost effective.

■ **Plan strategically for business development** – Tying up a significant amount of capital for no guarantee of return would have compromised Diva's existing plans for new business development.

■ **Stay focused** – If you need more than 50 words to describe your business you need to redefine your goals.

A clearly planned Business Strategy will anchor your commercial decisions and will keep you focused on your core business.

Your Business Strategy is a framework for decision-making that will help to keep your business on track.

Why do you need a Business Plan?

Planning ahead is vital to business success.

With a Business Plan you will:
- Anticipate risks and prepare for them
- Avoid expensive mistakes
- Consider all options
- Identify added value for your customers

Without a Business Plan you will:
- Take unnecessary risks
- Make expensive mistakes
- Underestimate your competitors' advantage
- Undervalue and possibly lose your customers

BUSINESS DISCIPLINE NO.2

BUSINESS PLANNING

BUILD YOUR BUSINESS

My objective in this chapter is not to explain in detail *how* to write a Business Plan, but *why* you need one – and to encourage you to ask yourself the right questions so that you review and use it regularly.

What are the benefits of business planning?

■ Your Business Plan works in partnership with your Strategic Plan (Business Discipline No.1)

■ Your Strategic Plan outlines the vision and the purpose that determines where you want to be in the marketplace

■ Your Business Plan ensures you plan ahead to achieve it

Mind the BOOM!

In sailing terms, the 'boom' is a pole that runs along the base of the sail to ensure that it maintains optimum shape and can guide the vessel in the direction that is required. It is a useful image to bear in mind, because your Business Plan is the boom that will provide similar strength and shape to the direction of your business.

As a mentor, I work with many business owners who avoid having to prepare a Business Plan simply because they don't really understand its purpose or how to put one together. I am here to tell you that it is really not that difficult. Like anything, if your plan is broken into manageable stages and tackled one step at a time – it is achievable.

What *is* a business plan?

Every business, no matter how large or small, will benefit from a Business Plan. It is a written document that acts as a reference point throughout the year. It reminds you of what you are trying to achieve, what resources you have, and what you need to achieve your aims. A good Business Plan will provide a *realistic* overview of your company and your objectives, strategies, financial forecasts and your place in the market. A Business Plan is *not* a public relations tool, although presentation is vitally important. It should be devoid of hype, rhetoric and unrealistic expectations.

Many business owners think of a Business Plan only as a financial document – something that outlines profit and loss, capital expenditure – or as a dreary obligation that needs to be prepared for the bank when extra finance is needed. Nothing could be further from the truth. Your Business Plan is the cornerstone of your future success. It is a plan of where you are now in relation to where you want to be.

Every successful venture begins with a clear vision and a detailed plan of action. Think of any goal you have ever strived for. The outcome depended upon a step-by-step strategy.

REVIEW, REVIEW, REVIEW
A Business Plan is an important review document. It provides a benchmark against which to assess and review ongoing results and assess how each business area is performing against forecast. It is especially important if you are an owner–manager who has no need to report to anyone, because it will keep you focused on your goals and steer you in the right direction.

A Business Plan IS NOT
a document prepared solely
in order to raise finance

A Business Plan IS
a detailed plan; a working
document; a road map to success

You will have taken stock of your skills and weaknesses, the competition, your environment, the risks involved, any regulations affecting your plans, and any financial outlay or rewards.

The process of compiling a Business Plan works along similar lines. It is a useful working document – and your detailed map of success. You need to review your progress in relation to the plan frequently and ask 'Why?' when the outcomes are not as you expected. If you plan carefully, review frequently and adjust your tactics, it will provide you with a unique guide to achieving the best possible results – hopefully ahead of the competition.

Why do I *need* a business plan?

Some entrepreneurs are business mavericks; they see the escape from the corporate maelstrom as an escape from regulation and accountability. They want great results but resist the control. But a lack of planning is an indulgence that very few can afford to risk.

If you work for yourself, you report to no one. You may be contractually accountable to your clients or customers but there is nobody to oversee your activity or to tell you what to do. If your sales are down you can *choose* not to do anything about the situation – or worse, you may not notice it. Before you know it you are drifting rather than driving your business. When problems hit, they can impact very quickly.

If you don't set down what you want to achieve, how can you assess your progress?

A carefully prepared Business Plan is important because it encapsulates your plans, aspirations and financial forecasts. It is your tool for reviewing your business. The review element is always important – but is absolutely *vital* if you work for yourself.

A Business Plan, rather like a satellite navigation system, can only guide you if you have told it where you want to go. Lack of planning leads to indecision; it means when the fog descends in the shape of a heavy workload and pressures on your time, there is a real danger you will lose sight of the big picture and be unable to find your way.

66

If you set out without a destination how will you know when you have arrived?

By compiling a Business Plan to cover a *fixed time span* of say, twelve months, you are also outlining the structure of your business and creating a framework for activity. Refer back to it on a regular basis to monitor your progress against your original targets. If you discipline yourself to get into the habit of reviewing every stage of your business *regularly*, the facts of the matter will make your priorities clear and you will get to know your business at the micro- and macro-level. The mantra is simple:

REVIEW, REVIEW, REVIEW – EVERYTHING YOU DO and then ALWAYS ASK THE QUESTION, 'WHY'?

Each element of your Business Plan will impact on other areas, which means that the results presented within one discipline will influence strategic decisions you make in the others. For example, sales that are lower than forecast will have an immediate impact on cashflow, which in turn will affect budgets for staffing and marketing, market position, expectations of growth, your exposure to risk and possibly your choice of suppliers or raw materials.

When you review one element of your business, it will influence the decisions you make in other areas.

The importance of asking 'Why?'

The business owner who reviews sales figures by looking *only* at the bottom line could spot something that *looks* like an increase against forecast and assume, 'I'm already on track and so I don't need to worry.' However, that kind of complacency leads to problems, as the simple example following shows.

The end-of-quarter sales at The New Computer Company total £12,000 against a target of £10,000. On the face of it, that seems an excellent result as the total is £2,000 up on target.

	Target	Actual
Total sales	£10,000	£12,000

However, an effective business forecast compiled as part of the annual Business Plan will include line-by-line *sales projections* for each retail outlet, which allows the business owner to check the figures closely and measure the outcome against the *original forecast*. On closer analysis, the results paint a worrying picture:

	Target	Actual
Customer A	£5,000	£12,000
Customer B	£3,000	£0
Customer C	£2,000	£0

All the sales came from Customer A.

The reality is that The New Computer Company is now extremely vulnerable, because two core customers haven't delivered on target. This leaves the company overly dependent on a single source of revenue. The following questions need to be asked:

What has gone wrong?
- Why haven't Customer B and Customer C placed orders?
- What is the true cost of Customer A increasing their order?
- What is the impact on the sales team if two key customers aren't ordering?

What can we do to about it?
It is unwise to spend further money on marketing without really understanding what went wrong or where your future revenue is

going to be coming from. The key point is that you should always look at everything that is happening in the context of what is happening within the other Business Disciplines as well.

A well-formed Business Plan can help you to spot trouble before it happens – by alerting you to the way the marketplace has changed, by identifying potential cashflow issues through the year, or anticipating future staffing requirements. It can also help you to stay ahead of the market and ensure that every decision you take is the right one to keep you on track.

When should I create a business plan?

There are no set rules about when to write a Business Plan. My own view is that it is unwise to start up a company without one. As the saying goes 'The road to Hell is paved with Good Intentions'.

Never assume that all is as it seems – especially if something seems too good to be true. Always ask the reason, 'Why?'

Hell in this instance is the gradual muddle and meltdown that is likely to result if you only ever 'intend' to write a Business Plan and you lose sight of where your business is heading.

Once you are up and running, it takes self-discipline to put time aside to review your business regularly – but I strongly recommend that you do. You will be amazed at how much clearer your thinking and decision-making become as a result.

Remember – the primary purpose of your Business Plan is as *a review document.* To be an effective working tool, it needs to be used proactively to plan ahead and reactively to monitor results.

I also recommend that you compile your Business Plan in consultation with your accountant and your solicitor, especially if you are planning to use your company name as a brand, or your goods are subject to intellectual property rights such as patents or trademarks. Their shared experience and perspective will be worth the modest investment.

> *"People who take professional advice at the business planning stage will spend less than they would on the cost of solving a problem later. There is also a time consideration: the management time involved in problem-solving distracts from core business priorities, and the stress involved is also a time stealer – it is time you can never recover."*
>
> **MARK J. CLARKE, SOLICITOR**

Who is my business plan for?

Your Business Plan is created primarily for you – to inspire you to review and run your business – and to help you to keep it in good working health. However, keeping your Business Plan up to date will also ensure that you are always in a strong position to talk to banks, investors and potential business partners. It's a good document in which to explain your objectives and to encourage everyone on your team to share the same priorities and goals.

Don't just work 'in' your business. Schedule time regularly to work 'on' your business too – the big picture is important.

Business plans come in all shapes and sizes. A sole trader with no employees who offers a single service will usually need a simpler plan than a limited company with several employees and an ambition to open offices nationwide. Whatever the size and aspirations of your business, the questions you need to ask yourself and the elements you should include in your Business Plan are the same.

Business planning will put the BOOM! back into your business sails – and your business sales.

70

9 principles of business planning

Typically there are nine sections in an effective Business Plan. The length and level of detail included in each of the sections will depend on the size, nature and scope of your business:

Section 1 Business overview

> A snapshot of the purpose of your business.

Section 2 Operational overview

> What your company produces and sells and how you deliver your product to market.

Section 3 Industry overview

> The state of the industry and your place within it

Section 4 Marketing overview

> A profile of your target market and people's buying habits.

Section 5 Financial forecasts

> An overview of cashflow, sales and costs.

Section 6 Management and staffing

> People, organisational structure, costs and training.

Section 7 Regulatory issues

> Intellectual property, health and safety issues and legal matters.

Section 8 Considerations

> Risks and other matters.

Section 9 Executive summary

> A one page summary outlining the conclusions and main benefits drawn from Sections 1–8. This section is often placed at the beginning of the report, although it is compiled last.

THE BOOM! BUSINESS TOOLBOX beginning on page 160 provides a step-by-step breakdown of the key purpose and benefits of each of the nine sections.

A snap shot review

This model of the essential relationship between your product, price, value and market is powerful in its simplicity and shows at a glance why so many businesses run into problems.

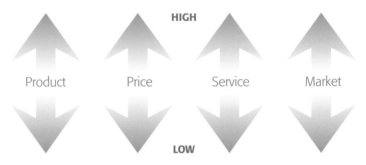

Four arrows – one direction

In essence, whatever kind of business you are in, you need to ensure that all four arrows are pointing in the same direction.

If all four arrows are pointing upwards, your business is likely to be successful.

For example – family-run business Crockett & Jones of Northampton has produced hand-finished high-grade shoes for four generations. The products are high quality and high priced; the company provides excellent customer service and sells to the top end of the market.

BUT – if one, two or three of the 'upward' arrows were replaced by a single downward arrow: poor product finish, low price, poor customer service, misjudged marketing – the business would suffer.

Waitrose, *Vogue* magazine and Porsche cars are similar examples of products or businesses that are successful because their product and pricing are in line with the expectations of their market sector. Customers are willing to pay the extra premium for what they perceive to be high-quality products or excellent service.

72

If all four arrows are pointing downwards, *your business is also likely to be successful.*

For example – the unstoppable success of Arthur Ryan's Primark retail chain is marked by the lowest prices on the high street and a wide range of ever-changing cheap and disposable goods. Their shoes are the antithesis of the Crockett & Jones range. Cheap materials, low production values, low price, fast checkout service, all aimed at the mass market, means that all their arrows point downwards – and they are a highly successful international business as a result.

BUT – if one, two or three of their 'downward' arrows were to be replaced by a single upward arrow: costly materials, high retail price, too much time spent serving individual customers, top-end marketing – the business could start to flounder.

Businesses such as Amstrad, EasyJet and Lidl are other examples of successful businesses that have targeted the cheaper mass market.

Common pitfalls

Many service industries create problems for themselves because they do not value their time accurately. High-quality service matched with a low pricing policy is a recipe for disaster.

Many goods manufacturers don't keep a close enough eye on their production costs and compensate either by under-pricing and eating into their profit margin, or over-pricing and failing to sell the goods.

Ask yourself:
- Which way do the arrows point in your business?
- Are they all facing in the same direction?
- If not – what steps do you need to take to put matters right?
- Is your business still viable?

If you are new to business planning or hadn't realised until now the importance of spending time on planning your business, Part three (page 160) will provide you with the starting point you need to gather your facts and focus on writing a thorough Business Plan, in nine sections.

A completed Business Plan adds validity and focus to your work and your priorities. You will feel empowered by your conclusions and they will focus you to drive your business forward.

A word to the wise

The most important characteristics of a viable financial plan are realism, honesty and accuracy. There is no point in fudging the facts, bluffing your cashflow or being over-optimistic about your expectations. Money doesn't lie. Hard cash is either there or it isn't. You can't conjure it up out of thin air or spend it more than once, and exaggerating your prospects for success is likely to cost you more than you will gain.

Review, review, review – again

Business planning is an ongoing process that always starts and ends with a review. It is as essential to your planning process as a production schedule or your bank statement. Reviewing every element of your business on a regular basis is important for four main reasons:

1 Things change – The market may change. You need to review your plans to know whether you are still on course.

2 We learn from our mistakes – Reviewing progress is important so that we can avoid repeating past mistakes and can adjust plans to get back on track.

3 Successes are worth repeating – It can be a great boost to commercial confidence to be reminded that your business is growing to plan and knowing your strategy is working.

4   Keep the big picture in mind – Every decision you make at the micro-level in business should be made with the big picture in mind. Think about the ramifications across all 7 Business Disciplines.

Knowledge is power; and the better you know your business, the better your end-of-year results will be. Too often those who don't plan ahead feel a sense of disappointment at the end of the financial year. The more knowledge you can glean about your competitors, your capabilities and your weaknesses, the stronger your Business Plan, and the better able you will be to adjust the future direction of your business and set a steady course to sail ahead of the pack.

'If it ain't broke don't fix it' – but if it is broke keep reviewing and revising until you get it right.

Planning a secure future

George Whitmarsh, MBE, is Managing Director of Global Integrity Ltd. He adapted his Business Plan to align with his company values.

"Global Integrity is an international company specialising in risk mitigation and security management. When I started the business I was quietly confident in my own ability and experience. I knew most aspects of the security industry inside out and I knew what I wanted to provide as a service. But having been in the military for almost thirty years I also knew I wasn't as business savvy as I needed to be.

My priorities
■   Deciding whether there was a major advantage in becoming a limited company (I was reluctant)
■   Choosing whether to rent new office space (too expensive?)

- Planning when to invest in sales staff, new technology and training facilities (a primary aim)
- Differentiating our services from those of our competitors (a value-driven goal)

Emma stressed the importance of first reviewing the benefits of each of these outcomes in relation to the core objectives outlined in my Business Plan. Business plan? I knew I had filed it somewhere …
Of course, all the issues were interrelated.

The outcomes and benefits

My company name and branding are designed to be synonymous with quality of delivery combined with openness, honesty and integrity. It became clear that the leap to become a limited company was completely in line with my core values and would help to differentiate my offering from the darker side of the security industry.

I am probably more service-driven than money-driven by nature, so it would be easy to get caught up in providing 5-star service at the expense of my profit margins if I didn't keep an eye on sales targets and cashflow. In revisiting our pricing policy, I considered which services met the particular requirements of my 'A' list and high net worth clients. Total reliability and a bespoke service are the answers. My plan now is to get to a point where I can train my own people and run my own training courses. Premises with the facilities to allow us to deliver on our goals are now part of the forward plan and can be justified financially. We have moved to a business centre that offers reception and conference rooms, garages and workshops. The image and the facilities are consistent with the message that I want to put across – so worth the investment.

I can still operate by doing most of the work myself, so hiring permanent staff is the lesser priority in the short term. That will be on next year's Business Plan.*"*   **GEORGE WHITMARSH**

BOOM! BUSINESS BYTES

A Business Plan is a review document. It provides you with a benchmark against which to measure progress over a fixed time span and is important regardless of what stage of development your business is at.

Your Business Plan is a valuable tool for assessing and reviewing your business on a regular basis.

BOOM!preneurs have the discipline to allocate time on an annual basis to plan ahead, write down and focus on all areas of your business. Business planning will encourage you to identify and budget for business growth – by identifying those areas which are priorities for development and others that could wait until a following year.

- **Prioritise and focus** – on your business objectives.
- **Recognise your strengths and weaknesses** – if you learn when to take advice from others you will speed up your decision-making and may gain a professional advantage.
- **Review progress on a regular basis** – to keep you on budget and your business on track.
- **Plan ahead** – in order to learn from past mistakes and always keep the bigger picture in mind.
- **Use your business plan** – it is primarily for your own purposes but is also useful for investors, your accountant and your bank manager.

A Business Plan usually focuses on nine key areas. See part three for a breakdown of key points that should be included in each section.

Why is marketing so important for your business?

Managing your marketing outcomes will keep your strategy focused on success.

- Marketing ensures you communicate to the right customers in an effective way and gain maximum results.
- Without marketing no-one will know you exist – let alone what you do.
- A business without a marketing plan is like a boat without a rudder – it will drift without direction.
- Managing your marketing activity will lead you to assess what is going on in the marketplace and how it affects your business.

BUSINESS DISCIPLINE NO.3

MARKETING MANAGEMENT

MASTER YOUR MARKETING

The main purpose of marketing is to communicate. In business it is your route to letting current and future customers know who you are, where you are, what you do, and what benefit you are to them. Marketing activity will always represent a cost to your company – in time and/or money. So it makes sense to plan your objectives in advance.

This chapter explains the importance of managing your marketing activity and your marketing spend; it explains why every business needs it in some form; and most importantly, why all marketing activity should be reviewed, regardless of the level of expenditure.

Effective marketing turns business communication into commercial opportunity.

I will not be giving you strategies to market your product, or specific tactics to use. The choice of whether to use printed media (such as leaflets, brochures, mailshots), e-marketing (for example, website, e-mailshots, virals) or a combination of methods, will depend on what results you are trying to achieve.

How to make marketing BOOM!

Never be complacent in your approach to marketing. Even in times of economic downturn or when your sales are disappointing, it is important to allocate marketing spend and to plan to do *something* each month. Your activities don't have to cost you a fortune. It is vital to *keep* communicating and not to assume that if customers have used you in the past they will do so again. Remember – your competitors are marketing to your clients too. Don't let them get the upper hand. However, before you spend a single penny, first ask yourself:

- What results am I looking for?
- Who do I want to talk to – and why?
- What do I want to say – and why?

Only once you have assessed the 'who's, the 'what's, and the 'why's can you decide on the 'how's – your tactics and your budget:

- What form of marketing campaign is best
- What level of budget to allocate to the task

Marketing is exciting because even the smallest change in your approach can bring about positive results. When marketing is well planned and well executed, the results can have a very positive impact on the company's profit and can help to avoid erratic cashflow. Yet each year companies squander thousands of pounds on poorly devised marketing strategies that fail to set realistic objectives or measure outcomes. Why? Too many businesses focus solely on planning marketing tactics, rather than first asking what they want to achieve.

I have worked with many business owners who will happily tell me that they have completed various sorts of marketing activity; but I rarely get a clear answer when I ask them to explain the rationale for the tactics used or what they achieved.

THE 'PURPLE COW' EFFECT
In the current marketplace it is no longer enough to just be competent or adequate at what you do – true success comes from being noticed as being remarkable. Marketing guru Seth Godin refers to this as 'purple cow' philosophy: the idea being that it is hard to tell one cow from another within a herd – but a purple cow will stand out immediately as being different and memorable. Of course, standing out will only get you so far. You need then to prove that all aspects of your business expertise and delivery are exceptional. Every business has the opportunity to create exceptional presence.

A well-considered marketing plan supports steady business growth and ensures you attract the right customers to your business.

Seek customer feedback

Peter Read is an insurance professional with ambitious plans for business growth. He needed to develop a marketing strategy to support his plans. His lack of marketing experience was making him cautious. He needed greater visibility for his company so we developed a basic plan.

"After three years in business I was seeking guidance on how to grow and develop my commercial insurance business. When I began working with Emma I expected her to start by encouraging me to spend money on advertising; instead she recommended that I consider very carefully what outcome I required – to increase turnover, increase my customer base, increase our professional reputation, and so on. I wanted all those things, but I specifically wanted to increase the top 20 per cent of my client base (the high-value accounts). Once I was able to identify my ideal customers, we were able to start discussing a strategy that would deliver.

I needed to understand what had prompted my existing clients to join my company in the first place, and why they continued to give me their repeat business. At Emma's suggestion, I sent out customer questionnaires – with an incentive to encourage completion (I offered to make a charitable donation for every questionnaire returned). I was amazed at the response rate and also pleasantly surprised by the comments made. It was gratifying to find we were considered honest, open and friendly; and working *on behalf* of our clients, rather than trying to make a quick profit.

This validation made me realise that investment in a website was essential as the most direct way of providing customers with information about our services, complete with the new testimonials offering credibility and a visual representation of our values. This tactic, supported by a mailing campaign, has already helped me to convert dozens of new enquiries into profitable business." **PETER READ**

Effective marketing is less about size of budget and more about knowing your market.

Don't rush ahead with marketing ideas until you have considered carefully what you want to achieve and who you want to reach. Remember: marketing requires effort so be sure to concentrate your effort on the areas that will deliver results.

Creating a marketing plan

Most entrepreneurs want their business to grow and all businesses need customers. The more ambitious your plans for business growth, the more customers you will need to attract. At the heart of your growth strategy will be your marketing plan. It is your strategy for attracting attention, increasing sales, getting your message across to new customers and reminding existing customers that you are still their preferred supplier. You need to consider very carefully:

- Your goal (the outcome required)
- Your strategy (your chosen media for delivery)
- Your tactics (your marketing tools)
- Your budget (how much you will spend)

Your goal – the outcome you want to achieve

Of course you want to make money, but what are your other, more strategic, goals? (Increasing your company's profile, increasing your mailing list, reminding customers you exist, data capture and so on). Your desired outcomes need to be specific.

Your strategy – how you are going to achieve it

Do you know your target market? You can't devise your strategy until you understand exactly who your customers are. Take some time to build a profile of your typical customers: who they are, what they do and how you could connect with them. Examine their needs and decide *why* they would want to buy *your* core products or services. What particular benefits do you offer that are unique? Do your research carefully and figure out how you can make approaches to this market sector. Be specific. A 'catch all' approach to marketing, with no particular customer in mind, will produce disappointing results that are neither cost-effective nor promote customer loyalty.

Your tactics – your marketing tools

There are many different routes to market. It may sound obvious, but it is important to choose ways that communicate most directly with your core customers. How much understanding do you have of networking, online marketing and search engine optimisation, direct mail, advertising or PR campaigns? Do you need to grow business locally or is your market national?

Consider taking strategic and practical guidance from a marketing agency or consultant if required – however, to achieve the best outcome, be extremely clear about your goals and target market before you brief them. Provide a description of a typical customer profile; explain the factors that influence their buying decisions and so on, so that you help the professional marketer to help you. (Make sure that the consultant's business background and experience match your needs as well.)

Your budget – your cash control

Your Business Plan (see Business Discipline No.2) will include an allocation for annual marketing spend. Keep a close eye on your annual budget as well as your campaign budget to ensure that you do not spend more than you can afford. It is a good idea to cost each element of each campaign separately so that you can track, monitor and later review all expenditure associated with each campaign. Include the cost of your time and any financial outlay. Remember to include in your cashflow and expenditure forecasts a monthly estimate of marketing expenditure – and amend your forecasts if any timings change.

Consider too, what you can do for little or no financial outlay. Marketing doesn't need to be expensive to be effective – and it always pays to think creatively about solutions. Consider reciprocal marketing: find a non-competing business that targets the same pool of customers, which has similar ethical values or offers a complimentary product range. If you can build a trusting working relationship, it may be feasible to create joint marketing promotions – sharing customers and costs.

The marketing calendar

On the next page is a marketing calendar. It is a simple planning model for tracking marketing activity. Every business would benefit from having something like this.

The headings can be altered in line with any special requirements for your business, but keep them as simple as possible. A straightforward form that is quick and easy to complete, and can be easily understood, is more likely to be kept up to date.

This simple format will encourage you to plan ahead and think about balancing your marketing activities across a twelve-month period. It will ensure that you plan the timing of your activities and that key events complement each other – which helps when coordinating the development of marketing materials too. Irrespective of the size of your business or the size of your marketing budget – you always need to develop a clear and focused plan.

How to use the marketing calendar

In the left-hand column, list the kind of marketing activity that is most appropriate for your business. The months of the year are marked to indicate how often the activity should take place. In this case:

	Jan	Feb	Mar	Apr	May	Jun	Jul	Aug	Sep	Oct	Nov	Dec
Networking	✓	✓	✓	✓	✓	✓	✓	✓	✓	✓	✓	✓
Exhibitions				✓					✓			
SEO/PPC Web campaigns	✓	✓	✓	✓	✓	✓	✓	✓	✓	✓	✓	✓
Leaflets			✓			✓			✓			

Track marketing activity by using a simple calendar.

- **Networking** – occurs monthly
- **Exhibition attendance** – twice annually
- **Search Engine Optimisation (SEO)/Pay Per Click (PPC)/ Web campaigns** – monthly
- **Leaflet mailings** – three times a year to coincide with key points in the commercial year

Of course, every business is different, so I am not recommending this schedule of activity as a model for all companies.

Marketing activity should always be proactive, not reactive.

Marketing outcomes

One of the fundamental principles of the 7 Business Disciplines is to always begin with a review: of your intentions, actions and outcomes. When it comes to planning your marketing strategy, it is vital to start with the end in mind. Set your goals and your expectations from the outset. Ask yourself:

- What would be a good outcome from each activity?
- What would be an excellent outcome from each activity?

Review each activity regardless of cost. Ensure that you set a timeframe for your expected return on investment and know what you expect to achieve. Include activities with minimal investment where your time is involved, such as networking and breakfast clubs.

If something isn't working, stop doing it or modify it. For example, if after six months of attending a regular networking meeting you have not won any business leads, you need to decide whether it is still worth attending. Your time is valuable and could be spent elsewhere – somewhere that may generate sales or profit.

Businesses that fail to grasp the importance of the review stage and make time for it are more likely to repeat bad decisions or be surprised when activities flounder or fail. Too often, small companies get caught up in the creative process and allow insufficient time to review the return on investment.

Your time is your money.

How to map marketing outcomes

I recommend the use of a simple marketing review for each activity you undertake. Even a free networking event should be measured in terms of whether it was a worthwhile use of your time and how it could be made more worthwhile next time around. Make sure your time is well spent; your time is *your* money and can be easily wasted.

Marketing activity	
Description	
Date	
Cost	
Good outcome	
Excellent outcome	
Actual outcome	

Review marketing outcomes by assessing expectations in advance.

- **Row 1: Activity description** – A one-liner to describe the action together with any reference code.
- **Row 2: Date** – The date you plan to launch the activity.
- **Row 3: Costs** – Your costs include personal time and the cost of production.
- **Row 4: Good outcome** – What you perceive to be a good outcome.
- **Row 5: Excellent outcome** – What you perceive to be an excellent outcome.
- **Row 6: Actual outcome** – The actual result.

Take stock of:

- The cost in time, effort and cash
- Whether the marketing approach was the best choice
- Whether the marketing materials were appropriate or effective
- Whether your expectations were realistic
- Whether it would be worth repeating the exercise; or whether your resources would be better allocated elsewhere

Careful assessment of each outcome will tell you what you should do or shouldn't do in future, as the following example demonstrates.

The Welly Garden Company

The goal

To increase the number of hours worked per day (from five hours to eight hours) and eventually the number of days.

The target outcome:

- Increase turnover by 60 per cent within twelve months.

The strategy

To obtain four new contracts for gardens half an acre in size that can be maintained in three hours per week.

The target market:

- Working families and retired people in the Sandbanks area of Dorset (average house worth £700,000, with large garden).
- Typically the home-owners can't or do not want to spend time gardening at the weekend.
- They have high expectations of having a beautiful garden that is perfectly maintained.

The tactics

Activity One: March (beginning of Spring)

The marketing tools:

■ A four-colour leaflet highlighting the unique service, with photographic examples of work, including customer testimonials and pictures of the team.

■ A door-to-door drop of 500 leaflets in areas of high net worth where houses have large gardens. (Repeat in May.)

Activity Two: April (Easter edition)

The marketing tools:

■ Create advertorial content for local 'society' magazine, highlighting differences between the Welly Garden Company and other local garden maintenance businesses.

The budget

A total of £2,000

Costs:

1,000 leaflets (A4 – four-colour print)	£750
Leaflet drop	£200
Advertorial (2pp) in local magazine	£1,050

Changing tactics

Marketing doesn't always need to be expensive but it has to be effective. It also needs to deliver results, to improve bottom-line profits. To spend money on marketing without reviewing previous outcomes is commercial folly. Analysing the results of your previous campaigns enables you to understand what went well, what didn't and which tactics delivered the greatest increase in sales and profit. You can decide more accurately whether you would want to repeat the activity or take a different approach.

Marketing activity	
Description	Leaflet drop to 500 homes Advert in local 'society' magazine
Date	1) March 2) April
Cost	Leaflet – printing and creative costs: £750; home drop: £200. Advert – creative costs: £300; media insertion: £750.
Good outcome	Increased awareness within targeted geographical area 20 enquiries from combined marketing activity Conversion to 4 new contracts at 3 hours per week.
Excellent outcome	30+ new enquiries, with conversion to 10 new contracts; resulting in the need to work an additional day per week throughout the peak gardening season.
Actual outcome	25 enquiries from combined activity, 6 new contracts. Conversion rate lower than expected – need to review process and find out why new business is not being secured.

■ Even when your campaign doesn't turn out as expected, review *all* aspects of the marketing outcome before dismissing any promotional activity – particularly if important elements are in line with your market position.

■ Take time to consider what could be done differently to ensure a better result.

■ It is your attitude towards doing things 'better' next time that will determine future success.

Make sure that your marketing strategy does you proud. Build a marketing plan that targets the right kind of customers for your business and sends out a powerful message about your values and competence, in a consistent and excellent way.

The following example of the Forever Green Café is an important illustration of why financial considerations alone do not provide the whole answer.

Bag it up

The Forever Green Café had been running for eighteen months. The owners took an ethical approach to food production and focused on using local organic suppliers to supply produce for their sandwiches. They wanted to draw more attention to the green credentials of their business to bring in new customers and decided to introduce a re-usable sandwich bag made of biodegradable packaging from sustainable sources. Customers would receive 10 per cent discount off their purchases each time they returned a bag. The bags were well received by customers but their production, combined with the discount, cost a lot of money. The question was – *Had it been worth the investment?* They reviewed the outcomes and asked themselves:

■ *Had they seen an increase in business?* Yes they had.
■ *Were people coming back more regularly?* Yes they were.

- *Were people reusing the bags?* Some of them were.
- *Did they make money out of it?* No they didn't. Although sales went up, there was no increased profit, as the bags had cost £2,000 to buy.
- *Did that mean they shouldn't repeat the bags?* Assessed solely from a financial standpoint, they should *never* do it again – but because the bags sent out an environmental message in keeping with their Business Strategy (Business Discipline No.1) they decided that they *would* repeat the investment.

So the question then became – *How could they do things differently to achieve a more profitable outcome?* They approached local organic suppliers to ask them to sponsor the bags so that the cost of the bags was covered by advertising and didn't cost the café any money at all.

The activity was repeated and was a suc-cess, from both the point of view of positioning and also financial return. This time, the cost of the bags was nil, so all turnover and result-ing profit made an immediate impact on the bottom line. Interestingly, the results on both

Make sure that all of your marketing efforts are focused consistently on the same target market.

promotions were virtually identical, which suggested that their initial expectations were too high – useful knowledge when planning promotional activity for the following year.

The core lesson here is that if you have researched your target market, are clear about the outcome you want and are sure of the message you need to convey – sometimes you simply have to bite the bullet and take a risk.

If you are in business, you can't afford to be modest about your skills or achievements. Whatever your budget and whatever your message, it needs to be consistent – and it should also reflect your company values. Always start with the outcome that you want firmly in your sights.

Plan to expand

Barbara Cox is MD of the award-winning company Nutrichef.

"Nutrichef had a whopping first year and achieved about £220,000 from start-up. The company has grown steadily from there year on year. We have eleven core staff and during seasonal peaks may employ up to twenty people. The business is established and doing well; but I have an ambition to take some of our flagship products to the general market. We are launching our flapjacks initially; and have plans to go international with the brand.

Marketing is Emma's core expertise and she encouraged us early on to develop an affiliate marketing scheme, now called the 'Friends of Nutrichef'. As a result we have commissioned a professional database which now has thousands of live contacts and customers and is an invaluable marketing resource.

More recently I have worked with Emma to rehearse and refine my sales pitch in order to be fully prepared for any questions a buyer can throw at me. It has made an immense difference to my confidence and the quality of my delivery.

The value of working with a mentor has been the increased speed with which I have been able to learn and take our marketing forward. For example, Emma helped me to drill down my costings and focus on pricing: to understand the importance that every .01 pence per unit has on the overall price of a our flapjacks and how important that actually is. We already have 70 outlets ready to take them and we need to get the financial detail right as well as the marketing strategy.

When you win a big award, you've got to work hard to maintain your market position and push yourself even more; because people expect more of you."

BARBARA COX

BOOM! BUSINESS BYTES

Marketing is the activity that makes your company visible and tells the marketplace what you have got to offer. It takes many forms, encompassing advertising, PR, mailings, e-marketing and overlaps with sales

Your marketing tactics should tell the world you have something unique or remarkable to offer.

tactics and customer service. As an effective BOOM!preneur you market your company every time you introduce yourself to someone and tell them what you do. Marketing needn't cost the earth – but it does need to be carefully planned to be effective.

- **Keep tight control over your marketing budget** – planning a careful strategy will give you an advantage over your competitors.
- **Review marketing activity** – taking stock of which activities work and which don't will save money as well as increasing commercial advantage.
- **Keep track of results** – by using and updating a simple marketing calendar.
- **Monitor investment** – before allocating marketing budget, review previous results to avoid repeating mistakes.
- **Plan ahead** – include your marketing plan in your annual business planning and keep your budget under review and under control.
- **Know your ideal outcome** – always know in advance what the preferred outcome would be.

When a company with the BOOM! factor has ambitious growth plans that require significant marketing outlay it can be valuable to work with a business mentor or a marketing consultant to help plan your strategy and save on costs.

How frequently should you monitor your finances?

- Monitor your sales, cashflow and cost control as often as your business requires.
- Keep your cashflow, costing sheets, bank balance and sales forecasts up to date on a daily basis.
- Help your accountant to help you by sending updates regularly.
- Make sure your profit & loss accounts, balance sheet, VAT and income schedule are filed promptly.

PRACTICAL FINANCE

MANAGE YOUR MONEY

I am matter-of-fact in my approach to finance. It is really very simple. In order to make a profit, you need to have more money coming in than going out. You also need to have a broad enough spread of customers, supplying you with enough steady income, to ensure that you are not vulnerable if one or two disappear.

Facing up to facts

Practical financial management on a regular and frequent basis is vital for business success. Focusing on the financial facts in three core areas of your business will snap all the rest of your priorities into focus:

Focus firmly on financial facts.

- ■ **Cashflow** – know what monies are coming in and out of your business
- ■ **Sales analysis** – plan your sales forecast and monitor actual sales
- ■ **Cost control** – manage your costs from the planning stage onwards

This chapter is *not* about the nitty gritty details of compiling a profit and loss account; it won't explain a balance sheet and there is little mention of VAT or taxation. Every business requires financial input from a professional and I recommend that you find one who can help you to ensure that your financial system is fully compliant with legal requirements. If you choose an accountant who can advise on financial strategy as well as finance, you will also get advice on the most cost-effective methods for managing your business.

My aim in this chapter is to ensure that you don't adopt a 'head in the sand' approach to money and that you understand the importance of the state of your finances. This business discipline is the most vital of the seven in terms of measuring the level of your success.

As an owner–manager it is crucial that you know *right now* what state your finance is in – and that you already know how it will look in the weeks and months ahead. If you can keep tight control over your cashflow, sales and costs, you will develop a much deeper knowledge and understanding of your business as well as being in a stronger position to weather the tough times and capitalise on periods of growth.

You will still need an accountant to manage your accounts and an accounts package to provide a picture of the financial state of your business (at any given time, to the end of last month, or last year end); but as a proactive business owner you also need to focus on now and on the future.

Remaining constantly aware of the state of your finances is a vital part of being in business. Only by monitoring the figures will you be in control. Use current *and* previous years' figures – so that you can consider them in context.

> *Don't ever, ever relinquish financial control of your business.*

There are so many excuses to choose from of course: *'Someone else does the books.' 'I don't understand numbers.' 'I'm too busy with everything else I have to do.'* Or even worse, *'The system looks after itself!'* Make no excuses. Delegating the task of keeping your system up to date is fine; but letting go or ignoring finances is simply not going to work if you want your business to be successful.

Wake up to finance

I take a very practical approach towards managing money and I focus on the detail. I learned the hard way at an early age that your bank balance doesn't take account of monies that have not yet cleared and since that time I have relied on my own methods to monitor cashflow – as an adjunct to the service that an accountant provides.

Cash is a measure of the financial situation right now. Management accounts report on what has passed. Both are of equal importance in running a business.

Business requires positive cashflow. It doesn't matter what kind of business you are in or how profitable it is, if you run out of cash, your business will struggle to carry on. Cashflow needs to be monitored at every stage – and when you are keeping your cash under control it is liberating. It takes the fear out of finance and leaves you feeling in control and positive about your business potential – even when your profits are low.

The easiest and most efficient way to monitor your finances is to set up a spreadsheet system that you can refer to; organised simply so that it is easy to update regularly and linked – to monitor cashflow, costs *and* sales. That way, every time you make a change to one sheet, the spreadsheet will reward you quickly, by showing the impact and knock-on effect of any unforeseen cost to the whole business. You will be able to anticipate problems before they happen. It goes without saying that the figures must be kept up to date on a regular basis. It is also *vital* to include every single cost within the business otherwise it won't show you an accurate picture.

Keeping your cash under control is liberating.

To gain the greatest benefit from your cashflow analysis it is wise to consider it in relation to your Business Plan (Business Discipline No.2) referring specially to the section on financial forecasting in part three (page 175).

Every business should have a cashflow forecast. In a company that is well-organised it will be revised regularly. Cashflow monitoring and analysis is part of the process of keeping your annual forecast up to date. If you don't have a forecast, the whole system falls down because you are not gaining knowledge about your overall performance: you won't understand your performance in the context of your plan, or the industry as a whole.

■ It is important to stress that if you haven't prepared a Business
■ Plan you are neglecting it at your peril. I would recommend that
you book time in your diary to begin one right now. Yes, right now.
At the very least you need to have prepared financial forecasts.

Tracking cashflow

When I first set up in business I didn't invest in an accounts
package. I didn't need to. Our invoicing system was very simple
and our company was very small. Our turnover in the early
days didn't warrant employing a full-time book-keeper; so we
contracted the work out. It is a common business model. The
arrangement freed up my time and conformed to my belief that
it's often better to ask an expert than to tie up your own time.

The book-keeper was home-based and worked using an
accounts package that was compatible with my accountant's. This
meant I had no direct access to the figures. The moment she took
the latest batch of invoices off-site, I felt uneasy
because I didn't have a clue what the latest
financial picture was.

*Log **all** your costs
daily for totally
accurate results.*

I needed to devise a control mechanism,
so I set up a spreadsheet that listed everything
that was going on in the business: all the financial incomings and
outgoings – including forward projections. I had other spread-
sheets for sales forecasts, costings and the bank balance. All were
linked together so that I could see precisely what profit we were
making and how much cash we had at any time.

Why did I set it up? I wanted to know *exactly* how each area
of the business was doing on any day and at any time. It worked
– and I loved it! It became such a useful tool that I have never had
to learn another method. My team at Diva Cosmetics have clear
memories of its effectiveness and many of them now use their
own variation in their current walks of life.

The Diva spreadsheet

Rachel Beresford joined Diva as the office accounts manager in 2002. She maintained the accounts within the business and made sure that cashflow and invoices were kept under strict control and that everyone was paid on time.

"Emma's spreadsheet was an excellent resource for monitoring cashflow. It didn't replace an accounts system, but it was an invaluable analytical tool. It listed all suppliers and all customers; I then added all orders, all invoices, all bills, all monies in, all monies out as soon as they arrived.

For example, if invoices worth £100,000 were issued on 3 March, the spreadsheet would show the financial impact in thirty days' time, or whenever those invoices were due for payment. It acted as a rolling financial forecast for the whole year and provided Emma with an exact picture of the Diva cashflow at any one time. We reviewed and updated it daily. When you are paying out sums in excess of £20,000 at a time to suppliers, you don't want any unpleasant surprises further down the line.

Emma didn't like people waiting for payment either. She wanted to make sure that other people were paid on time, just as she liked to be paid on time. There was always a great sense of fairness in her business dealings.

I have since created variations on Emma's spreadsheet for various other business-owners, such as sole-traders, who haven't invested in an accounts package. Keeping it up to date makes end of year accounts so much quicker and easier."

RACHEL BERESFORD

'Emma's spreadsheet is 100 per cent excellent as a method for reporting on and controlling the cashflow.'

! Never try to do without an accountant, and if your company is
■ large enough, invest in an accounts package that is compatible
with your accountant's – it will save you money in the long run.

In my work as a business mentor I am often approached by
business owners who are trying to juggle their management
responsibilities and are unsure where best to focus their efforts.
In most cases, initial efforts should be focused on sorting out the
finance, because with financial control comes business control.

As I say in my talks, if you *ever* rely on getting a text or letter
from your bank to discover that you are overdrawn – you are not
managing your business effectively and you should feel embar-
rassed. It is important always to take control *before* things turn
sour. Take control of your finances and others will have confidence
in you. Speak to your bank about issues before they happen. It is
the small changes that make a big difference over time.

Reversing fortunes

**Sarah Isaacs is a solicitor who took over the ownership of her law
firm two years ago.**

"At the time I took over the ownership of Kiteleys Solicitors the
company was in a very weak position commercially, and the general
mood was low. At Emma's suggestion I began by focusing on the
finances. I undertook a review of all the monthly outgoings; it was a
sobering and very disheartening experience.

The practice manager and I prepared a spreadsheet to review our
income and our expenditure over the year ahead and undertook a
cashflow analysis. The profound impact of the total, which showed
consistently negative cashflow, hit us with such a blow that we decided
immediately on some significant changes within the business.

- We took the decision to cut staff; an outcome which hit us hard on a personal level.
- We sold on work that ordinarily we would have retained. (As a result of relatively new changes to the law, solicitors can refer work to other practices and receive a fee for it. In effect, we presold some of our cases.) It was not our preferred option. Whereas each individual case might bring in income of £3,000 on average, we were able to sell on at only £250 - £500 a case.
- We sub-let a huge floor in our building to reduce our overheads and bring in rental income.

It was not a long-term strategy but it served to control our cashflow problem in the short- to mid-term and gave us time to plan ahead.

Having a business mentor was absolutely pivotal to our survival in those first twelve months and helped us to steer a steady course through the maelstrom of borrowing and negative cashflow. It was a horrendous time.

In spite of the challenges, especially the pain of making a valued member of staff redundant, we did increase our turnover during that first financial year – and we have since increased it by a further 10 per cent. It's quite a result, because at the time I took on the business we were showing a year-end loss of £25,000.

My experience has shown me that when you learn to understand the cashflow of your business on a micro-scale, it actually makes you appreciate everything that everybody does. And when people feel appreciated, things just work so much more efficiently. I can genuinely trace back the positive change in mood within the company, to the changes in our approach to financial planning."

SARAH ISAACS

Sales analysis

During the business planning stage you will have prepared a sales forecast. This document should be prepared in quite a lot of detail (Business Discipline No.2), to include a breakdown by month of your anticipated sales. The greater the level of detail you include when you first draw up your plan – the greater control you will have overall (provided you keep it up to date of course!)

I recommend that a sales forecast should be broken down into the different *types* of business you offer. For example:

■   If you run a service industry that sells items too – prepare a separate breakdown and forecast for each category.
■   If you run a sales company – do an analysis by each product and also by each customer. This will give you a more accurate picture that will also help with stock control, ordering and so on.

Your sales forecast should tie in with your cashflow forecasts so that you can determine how much money is likely to come in over the course of the financial year. It needs to be realistic and as accurate as possible.

When running Diva, I had a sales analysis spreadsheet which let me analyse and see at a glance how each of our customers were performing. The level of detail you include in your spreadsheet will depend on the type of business you are running.

I couldn't have managed my business without knowing this level of detail. Without detailed financial information, how can accurate decisions be made? It is important to keep asking:

■   If a customer is behind forecast – what has gone wrong?
■   Is it just a timing issue or was the sales forecast inaccurate?
■   What can be done to encourage further sales?
■   Is further investment in marketing needed, and if so, when? Now? In three months?

Always take time to check that the figures are absolutely accurate; if you neglect the figures, the whole process loses its value.

Cost control and controlling costs

Every product or service needs to be costed accurately so that you can set the selling price at a level that makes a profit. Everyone in business knows that – so why, why, why do people not get it right? Too many small businesses are running at a loss because their costings have not included all the variables and as a result they are under-charging for the final product or service.

At Diva we prepared a breakdown of costs for each product *before* presenting to a customer. The reason was simple. Customers always want to know what the price will be. You can't negotiate if you don't know the unit cost and whether it is cost-effective for you to take the deal!

Costing accurately is often the hardest part of a business to get right – regardless of whether it is a service- or product-based business. You can be sure that you will make many mistakes along the way, but if you continually review, assess and re-evaluate what you anticipate you *should* be making, versus what you are *actually* making, you can make changes before you have made too much of a negative impact on your business.

Diva costings

Diva's strategic statement pledged to, 'ensure the best choice possible on the high street.' That meant the best choice not only from a quality/design perspective but from a price/value standpoint too. We would have ruined our 'expert' reputation had we presented products to our customers without completing a costing exercise first. Costings needed to be affordable from our point of view (allowing enough profit to trade); but we also had to ensure that the

You need to analyse your costs to ensure that the actual spend and return are as accurate as you had estimated.

106

Prepare a breakdown of costs for every business activity before it is carried out.

RRP (recommended retail price) for each item was appropriate for the consumer market and at a unit cost that our customers could afford to purchase.

The proposed RRP was set at a level that would allow our customers to achieve their margin requirements (often as high as 70 per cent). It was quite a balancing act to ensure that everyone was satisfied – but approaching costs at a micro-level ensured Diva's profitability.

Analysing costs is not the end of your financial management. Planning to make a profit comes first, and then you need to make sure that you follow through – firstly to safeguard the overall success of the business; and secondly to check that you make a profit and are not repeating past mistakes.

The cost of a small concession

Profit margins are sensitive at the best of times, but are usually healthiest when there are economies of scale involved. The following tale will be familiar in principle to many and is intended as a reminder always to look at the big picture before agreeing to an unplanned request.

Diva would usually deliver goods to Claire's Accessories every two weeks. Each delivery comprised of a minimum of 2–4 pallets and, on occasion, took up an entire lorry load – this was the most cost-effective way of delivering stock. However, Claire's would occasionally request an interim delivery of 3–4 boxes of a single item – not even an entire pallet. Saying 'yes' would significantly impact on our profit.

Delivery Request	Quantity	Cost	Cost Per Unit
Every 2 weeks	2–4 pallets (30,000 units)	£450	£0.015
Special delivery	2–3 boxes (3,000 units)	£150	£0.05

On the surface, the cost of the extra delivery was only £150 and it would be easy to agree to it. However, when reviewed at a level that shows the impact on the unit cost, you truly understand the effect on the bottom line.

Sharing such detailed information with the entire Diva team was extremely empowering; everyone worked together to ensure that 'out of the ordinary' costs were minimised in order to contribute to Diva's profitable success!

Costings analysis

Kate Woolston joined Diva as a general assistant on the freight desk before becoming accounts manager.

"Emma had instigated a 'costings analysis' project at Diva, which I managed. It meant gathering vital information from all costings and amalgamating it in a single spreadsheet for detailed analysis.

The margins on individual items at Diva (such as lipsticks and eye shadows) were often small, although there was a threshold margin percentage per product that had to be achieved. As the classic 'middle men' in our deals – we managed production in the Far East but delivered to customers in the UK – we had very little room for error, and the difference between profit and loss could be marginal.

The cost analysis form was simple. It included all costs associated with a product, from manufacturing to shipping (including components, like labels and boxes). Contingency costs would be included as well to ensure we always made a profit. Costs were the driving force of the Diva business: our products had to be of good quality, but cheap enough and with great enough margin for the onward customer whilst still ensuring that Diva made a profit.

We checked final costs against the original estimate post-delivery, to check that all of our assumptions had been correct (cost per product for sea freight for example). This way we could decide easily whether or not to offer repeat business, or in which area of production we could shave costs.

It was a sales business, so the customers were always trying to squeeze a better unit price out of us. Being able to see from our costing sheets whether we could negotiate on price, or add a gold label or a different scent, was invaluable. It meant we could make decisions quickly and beat our larger competitors.

On the rare occasions when a delay in the Far East meant our goods missed their slot for shipping via sea freight, we could ascertain easily (using the costings sheets) whether we could afford to air freight and still make a profit; or whether it would be better to wait until the next shipment. They say the customer is always right and we did try to accommodate all needs, but at the end of the day you won't have a successful business if you don't make a profit – it is always a fine balancing act.*"*

KATE WOOLSTON

Accountability

Keeping accurate production costs is only one aspect of cost control. If other people within your organisation are authorised to spend money, it is essential that you put a monitoring system in place. You must know how much everyone is spending, on what, and when payment is due. This is of crucial importance with regard to your cashflow.

A purchase order system is a simple way of solving this. Each purchase should be signed off and approved, not only by the department manager but also the accounts manager.

You need to be able to cover your overheads. Make sure you include an element for running costs and other commitments on your costing sheet.

Taking control of the numbers

Senior staff may need some coaching in the basics of practical finance. Director of New Product Development, Nicky Connors, had to overcome her nervousness of numbers.

*"*When I was first asked to manage a budget, my initial feeling was fear and resistance. I lacked confidence with figures and didn't believe it was my role to manage money or to monitor critical spend. However, I simultaneously felt rather empowered by the task.

Emma would only accept accuracy and precision, so it was a big deal that she had faith in me to manage Diva's money for technical expenditure. I wanted to prove to her that I was worthy of being trusted. I developed my own systems of tracking expenditure and cross-referring costs. I used all sorts of different test methods where possible to save money. (Who doesn't want to see an annual spend come in under budget?) I found that it was actually an easy thing to do. As my awareness grew, I was better able to manage and track expenditure, and learned to argue with conviction when it was imperative that something had further investment.

This led to a greater ownership of my area within the business and gave me control of the technical process. It enabled me to see the entire product cycle, and how it had an impact on the business and profit margins as a whole. A really good idea, because the more profit we made at year end, the greater our financial rewards come bonus time!*"*

NICKY CONNORS

If your staff are held accountable for their own monetary spend, they are more likely to pay attention to what they are spending and to understand the impact of costs on the bottom line. Explain to people how to prepare costing sheets properly. If you take the time to do it once, you may never have to do it again. It's amazing what a difference in personal attitude can make to overall profit.

The Wimhurst way

Andrew Perriam has been my accountant from the first day I set up in business. As my mentor and sounding board he is integral to my business development strategy. Following is his view of the business owner–accountant relationship.

"To get the best from your accountant, a good relationship is vital and you must be in regular contact. Business owners should use their accountant as a sounding board, to challenge their plans and decisions. The perfect client is an excellent communicator and will be honest about what is really going on in his or her business.

Diva Cosmetics was a success for many reasons, but from my standpoint it was primarily because Emma communicated, regularly and openly. She also combined an in-depth understanding of how marketing worked with a brain that is wired for the detail of financial management. From day one she questioned, 'What level of profit am I achieving?' and expected me, as her accountant, to challenge her on the strategic issues within the business.

It's all very well selling lots of units, but it's important to stop and ask – what is the profit margin on those units? There is no point in taking on new business if it isn't going to make you any money.

The old adage is true: *Turnover is vanity – Profit is sanity*

A business is at a disadvantage if it relies solely on monthly, quarterly or year-end accounts. They won't give you the immediate picture. In contrast, the Diva cashflow system would show Emma at a glance:

■ What have I got coming in?
■ What's going out?
■ What have I got?

She made sure that she was never in for any nasty surprises and always stayed aware of the bigger, long-term picture.

I can remember playing a particularly key role when Diva started to import from Taiwan. We did a lot of work on the financial model: how to negotiate terms of payment, how to spread risk across the year and so on. It required negotiating an overdraft facility from the bank. Her excellent relationship with her bank helped enormously then, and again when she decided to sell Diva. The due diligence process was completed quickly and easily because the book-keeping and financial records were so consistent and transparent. "

ANDREW PERRIAM

BOOM! BUSINESS BYTES

A profitable business is, by definition, one that makes money – and a business that does not have its cash under control is likely to be added to the list of annual business failures. If you are in business you have no choice but to put a system in place to manage your finances efficiently. BOOM!preneurs recognise that financial management is the foundation stone of business control and growth.

■ **Face up to your cashflow** – and make sure you have an efficient system in place to manage your money on a day to day basis.

■ **Know your costs** – before you spend any money. Costing individual projects and keeping those costs under control are your keys to profitability.

■ **Maintain control** – hire a book-keeper, use an accountant, but never ever relinquish control of your finances.

■ **Learn basic facts** – what basic financial terminology means and make sure you know how to read a profit and loss sheet accurately.

■ **Encourage accountability** – explain financial terms to your team and involve everyone in the process of monitoring costs.

■ **Plan ahead** – always prepare a sales forecast as part of your annual Business Plan and keep in touch with how your customers are performing against target.

■ **Keep an eye on the bottom line** – in order to gain greater understanding of your business.

Managing finance is not rocket science. It is very simple to organise and is your key to running an effective and successful business.

If you don't keep your cash under control on a daily basis, sooner or later your costs will start to control you.

If you inspire others they will surprise you.

THE SOFT SKILLS

Business Disciplines No.5–7 focus on aspects of business management that are harder to control – the people-related areas. They are also the areas that are likely to provide the greatest personal satisfaction when you get them right.

My Business Disciplines No.5–7 will help you to communicate, motivate and improve the results of your team, your customers and yourself. These are the leadership disciplines that reflect your personal values and influence your management style in the daily running of your company.

If you **inspire others,** they will **surprise** you.

Why are people so important to your business?

Your people are your most valuable business resource.

■   **Matching** – The people you work with have the potential to make or break your business.
■   **Attracting** – Finding and keeping the right people takes time, effort and money so it important that they are a good 'match' for your needs.
■   **Retaining** – Losing staff is expensive, inefficient for service and production and lowers morale.
■   **Motivating** – Many businesses have top talent on tap yet fail to fulfil their potential because they don't want to invest in helping them to perform to their best.

TEAM BUILDING

INSPIRE AND LEAD
YOUR TEAM

Building a strong team is what really puts the BOOM! into your business. This relates to your employees and also to external support functions too – such as your accountant, lawyer, human resources consultant, PR or marketing team.

People management skills rarely come naturally, and most owner–managers find the recruitment and training aspects of running a business the most daunting. However, with careful planning, it is possible to make the process fairly simple yet deliver outstanding results. You just need total clarity regarding the outcomes required.

■ This section does not offer facts and details about recruitment practices, employment law, pension plans or other legalities. You will find all the information you need from internet resources, your accountant, solicitor or HM Revenue and Customs. Suffice to say that it is crucially important that before hiring anyone, you ensure that you know what terms of business are expected by law and that your business conforms to government recommendations.

Learning at the sharp end

I knew that human resource management and employment law were complex areas and that when I became an employer I would need to draw up a contract of employment and learn about tax codes and employee rights. However I had neither the time nor the inclination to gain overnight expertise. My mind had to remain firmly focused on growing and developing the business. So I took the decision to work with an employment expert right from day one. Yes, the cost was a consideration, but I knew that if I found the right advisor it would be a worthwhile investment. I believed that consulting someone who understood the intricacies and potential pitfalls of what I was embarking upon was very important in ensuring that I was creating a business that was compliant with legal requirements. I also wanted to establish good practice guidelines from the outset, laying down procedural foundations that would protect both my rights as an employer and my employees' rights as individuals.

My decision was one I have never regretted. My solicitor came highly recommended by a former colleague so I knew I could trust his professional advice. Both my solicitor and my accountant became an integral part of my business management team, which ensured consistency of approach and made my own role so much easier as the business grew.

The recruitment process

I devised a rigorous approach to recruitment. I knew I needed to work with people who had enthusiasm, sparkle, passion for the industry and a nose for detail – a team of people that I could relate to and rely upon. In truth, like most people, my eventual recruitment decisions were usually heavily influenced by my instincts – but supported by a three-stage interview process, so I could be sure that only the quality candidates would make it through.

A recruitment success story

I needed a marketing assistant from day one because I needed a creative expert, who understood how to create colour combinations and could devise make-up colours that were fashionable and wearable. I advertised and received over thirty applications.

"It is well worth consulting experts at the start-up stage of company development. To seek and consider appropriate advice from the outset is a strength. Emma's willingness to say, 'I need your guidance in this area.' is fundamental to her ongoing success. Her external advisors (solicitor, accountant) are always included in strategic meetings and she has the same expectations of her 'external' team as she has of those in-house."

MARK J. CLARKE, SOLICITOR

Stage 1 – I filtered out the definite 'no's initially, basing my assessment on the standard of the covering letter. Anyone who had submitted an application that included spelling mistakes (or who couldn't spell my name!), had illegible writing, or whose letter lacked substance was instantly dismissed as unsuitable.

Stage 2 – I interviewed ten people and selected a short-list of three to return for a second interview. I asked a valued friend and ex-colleague to sit in on the interviews to gain an alternative perspective. It is always good to have a second opinion.

Stage 3 – The appointment was an entry level position but as my first member of staff it was critical that I got this right, so two applicants were invited back for the final selection stage. They were given three days to prepare a presentation on 'Your understanding of the state of the teenage cosmetics market.' (No PowerPoint allowed!)

Nicky Connors became my first employee and she was definitely the right choice. Her presentation was outstanding, showing clear attention to detail and demonstrating a true passion for the industry. Nicky has a first class honours degree and had previously trained as a make-up artist. You might think that I would have selected her on her qualifications alone, but the most important selection criteria for me were: that she represented my values – crucial when meeting clients; and that we 'matched' – that is we could work together and that she was energetic.

It was the right decision. Nicky was an integral part of Diva's success. She grew in experience and status along with the business, and within three years became Director of New Product Development, with responsibility for design and development of all our lines.

120

The art of matching

'Matching' is a subtle process. It requires a meeting of minds, and energy levels, mutual respect, shared values, complementary skills, a willingness to forgive a few character flaws, and a sense of personal recognition – 'I like this person', 'I could work with that person', or 'This person is like me'. A perfect match in business needs also to be a match for the company culture and to blend with others in the company. But beware. You are not recruiting a best friend; you are recruiting a colleague, whose skill-set and future performance will contribute to the profitability of your company so it's crucial that you make the right recruitment decisions – they determine the success of all your activities.

If you are inexperienced in conducting interviews be sure to take advice, or involve a professional interviewer. Always ask for candidate references – even if you don't follow all of them up. The same applies when choosing suppliers – try always to find people who have been highly recommended by someone whose opinion you respect and whose business is similar to your own.

A not-so-successful recruitment story

I didn't always get it right. However, every situation is a learning situation, even if you learn what not to do!

Towards the end of Diva's first year of trading, we were experiencing rapid growth. My time was being stretched between two conflicting areas of responsibility: namely, new business development – a primarily outward-facing sales and relationships role; and business management.

I believed at the time that my priority was to remain focused on managing the operational side of the business and oversee-ing new product development. I decided to recruit a business development manager, to represent Diva and bring in new business.

It was a classic business mistake – and one which I come across on many occasions when I am mentoring. My business, like most start-ups, was based around my experience, my values and my wish to make my business unique. My company and I were one and the same. I *was* the business. You can instil those values into others over time but no-one else is going to be able to represent your ethos, vision and experience to new customers as effectively as you, especially during the start-up phase. I realized with great clarity that I was the best person to represent my business to new clients.

Not only did I make a mistake in the role I was seeking to fill but nor did I follow my proven three-stage recruitment method. I employed someone I already knew and from the moment she joined I realised that she was not a 'match' – neither in her experience nor in her approach to work. I took early advice from my employment lawyer and was able to rectify my mistake within her trial period. We parted company in a professional and law-abiding way.

A mistake is only a mistake if you don't learn from it. I definitely *did* learn. Until a company is big enough to adopt an identity that transcends the personality of the founder, it is important that the owner is personally involved in bringing in new customers. I also recognised the need to stick to a rigorous recruitment procedure; to ensure that I had clearly identified the skills and character traits required before advertising for a particular role.

The positive aspect of this episode was that I managed never to repeat the mistake again. Even as a business mentor I ensure that I am always an effective 'match' for my clients in both character and business ethos.

*Remember – you **are** your business.*

The people principles

There are three key principles for finding the right people and building an effective team:

- **Attract** – How to find and employ the right people
- **Retain** – How to keep people happy and incentivise them to stay with the company
- **Motivate** – How to encourage people to deliver, develop and grow

To ensure you make a good investment, don't compromise on your expectations. Your team is your most expensive resource and your most valuable asset.

A lesson in attraction

In order to attract the right calibre of candidate, you first need to know what you want: what you want the person to do, what skills you require, at what level, and in what salary range. In recruitment as in marketing, you need to plan for your preferred outcome *before* you place your advert and definitely before you interview. Your advert and your job description need to be so clearly focused that the right candidates recognise themselves and apply because they understand what you want.

- Determine the exact role you wish to recruit for – and clearly define areas of responsibility.
- Be clear about the skills that will be required to carry out the role and decide on the type of personality that will be the best fit for your team.
- Consider the needs and responsibilities of other employees. Who will the new person report to and work with? Who and what will they manage? Are the boundaries between roles and responsibilities clearly defined? Will their characters 'match'?

Honesty and clarity will ensure that you recruit correctly.

It is important to be really honest in interviews about what you are promising, what you are expecting and what you want people to do.

Too many people project their own values on to other people and see only what they want to see. If there are opportunities for career progression, then let the candidates know and gauge their reaction; if there aren't – don't imply there will be, or create a job title that makes the role seem more than it is.

Bear in mind that job titles and work hierarchies can cause controversy and dissent in the work place. Make sure that you have planned your reporting structure and your pay scales *before* you make an offer to your new recruit, so that your job offer is fair to other staff at the same level.

Clarity is important when retaining third-party suppliers too. Be clear, honest and open about your expectations and your style of working and find out about their payment structure and timing. Follow it up in writing, with a letter of agreement if necessary. This approach will save any misunderstandings at a later date.

"When I first met Emma I remember being impressed by her warmth. She was sincere and straightforward and very polite. She asked me whether I was interested in the position. I said, 'Yes, it sounds great to me' – and it did. Then she shocked me by adding, 'I'll tell you this now. I can be a bit of a nightmare to work for.' I was taken aback by her candour and wondered whether she was right, but thought, 'You can't get more honest than that!' She said, 'We work hard here. We get our work done – but we also have a lot of fun. It would be nice if you could join our team. Are you interested?' On the spot, she offered me £1,000 more per annum than I had asked for and included me within the bonus programme. I had never been so happy to get a job. She was tough but fair from the outset and I knew exactly what to expect."

RACHEL BERESFORD

124

Recruit to retain

Recruiting people is time-consuming and expensive, so the last thing you want is for valued staff to leave within a very short period of time after joining. Losing a key member of staff can be catastrophic for a small company, especially if you have only a very small team.

If your level of staff retention is on the low side (by which I mean people tend to leave within six months to one year) you need to review the reasons why, by asking some hard questions of yourself and others:

- Is the company perceived as offering job security?
- Does your selection process need review?
- Do your working practices and processes need review?
- Would a staff induction programme help?
- Was there a lack of clarity about the role?
- Did the job offered at interview differ from the job in reality?
- Are you expecting too much from one person/one role?
- Was the level of pay set at a fair level?
- Are the working conditions acceptable?
- Are the working hours too long?
- Is the job too challenging or not challenging enough?
- Does the office provide a pleasant working environment?
- Is your technology up to date and adequate?
- Is the company welcoming and supportive to new staff?
- Are there difficult personalities on the team?
- Are you a difficult person to work for?
- Do you need a human resources expert to help you to undertake a review of the company?

Ask the 'why's and then ask 'What can we do about it?' If someone resigns, invite them to an exit interview. Your existing staff may also be able to offer insight into any problems. Consider using a human resources consultant to review processes. Plan for change.

People need to feel valued and important to the team, no matter how long they have been with the company. It is surprising how easily this can be achieved – and often *not* at very little cost.

Don't let the good ones get away

In 2001 I was recruiting for a marketing assistant to do costing analysis and to help review the financial side of product development. I knew that I needed someone who would pay thorough attention to detail, who was experienced, enjoyed working with accounts and was motivated by profit.

A young graduate called Saskia was among the applicants for the role. I was immediately attracted to her enthusiasm and she definitely had a sparkle about her. I knew instantly that she would be an excellent 'match' for Diva. However, I also knew intuitively that she would absolutely hate the role, because it was detail-orientated and would not involve interaction with our clients. I chose my preferred person for the job, and turned Saskia down.

I thought that was the end of that. Wrong! Within two days Saskia wrote to me, questioning my decision. She felt that she was absolutely right for Diva and that I couldn't possibly *not* take her on!

I rang and offered her a job on the spot. She had demonstrated that she had an in-built tenacity that could not be taught. I knew that she would be an asset to the company and how right I was. Saskia went on to manage one of our biggest and most prestigious accounts with flair.

The business lesson was – yes have a plan, yes stick to your plan, but consider alternatives if they present themselves.

'Diva was a brilliant training ground. Emma was essentially a mentor to me, which played an important role in my career.'

SASKIA LANKSHEAR

126

Selecting and managing your team can have its ups and downs but the right people will become your most valuable asset.

Manage to motivate

When you run a small company there is rarely a budget allocated for staff training and development courses. It is therefore important that your employees are given sufficient time and support to enable them to learn on the job. In-house training will also enable you to gain some insight into their skills, aptitude and personal interests. Annual appraisals to discuss ambitions and aspirations are an important part of the motivational process.

Understanding what motivates each member of your team will help you to enhance their skills and experience to maximise performance. Insight into behaviour traits, confidence levels and management skills will enable team-building and staff development. Empowering your teams to take the initiative, generate new ideas and to take responsibility for their actions will also motivate greater productivity.

Appraisals

Annual appraisals are as important to the healthy running of your company as your annual Business Plan. When properly undertaken they provide invaluable feedback about your team and the company. Incorporated within the appraisal process should be individual development plans that allow each person to provide feedback and to focus on their future. The appraisal process should not be linked to salary and benefits.

Each member of your team should have a personal development plan (as part of your Business Plan) and job-related training should be available to all. Regardless of how many employees you have, treat everyone as an individual and you will benefit from the results.

An appraisal form doesn't need to be complicated. (There are many examples that can be downloaded from the Internet.) In my experience the completed form is an essential tool for effective management and the evaluation of staff performance. A team that improves at an individual level will also improve the productivity of the whole organisation.

Ask each individual member of staff to complete an appraisal form prior to the formal meeting – and then use their answers as the basis for discussion. Remember, this process is not about you, as the owner or manager, although you too should invite assessment from your team; it is about each individual member of staff.

Appraisals can be considered daunting, time-consuming and possibly stressful – but provided you have one-to-one meetings with each of your team members on a regular basis you will know what many of the issues are and can plan for them in advance. Having regular conversations about work, career, aims, progress and ambitions will ensure that the appraisal period is constructive and relaxed. If you feel uncertain how to conduct the process to greatest effect, consult a human resources professional for further advice.

Rewarding results

Personal motivation was one of the most important keys to Diva's success. Everyone in the company was given targets and objectives and there was also a bonus scheme. As a result everyone felt motivated, well rewarded and valued – most of the time. I never lost anyone because they didn't like the job. I made sure that I wove rewards, benefits and recognition into the fabric of the company and my team consistently gave their best, partly because I expected them to, but also because they wanted to.

"Emma worked tirelessly; she was enthusiastic and committed to doing everything well, and that rubbed off on all of us. I've really tried to adopt that 'can-fix' attitude to problems I've encountered since."

KATE WOOLSTON

Shared targets and objectives are an important aspect of management. They keep everyone pulling in the same direction and reinforce the fabric of the team. Different people are motivated by different outcomes, but I have learned that even those who are more motivated by people than profit will feel very positive about receiving a productivity bonus!

Your out-of-house team will benefit from encouragement too – and will be motivated by your enthusiasm, focus, communication and willingness to pay on time.

"Prompt invoice payment is a great motivator for self-employed professional staff. It's a very important point. Late payments do nothing to generate good will. Prompt payments will make a good working relationship even better."

MARK J CLARKE, SOLICITOR

The best form of motivation, however, is to lead by example. As a business owner and employer you are more than simply an individual running a business; you are the reason that this particular group of people is coming to work each day and getting paid at the end of the month. There is no switching off from that. We spend more time each day with colleagues than we do with our own families a lot of the time, and your team will be looking to you for inspiration, energy and direction. The expectation can be tough when you are having an 'off' day.

"Emma was extremely driven and expected you to be driven too, but she would always show her gratitude to the team and reward us handsomely with praise, or something that would regenerate the team spirit. That compensated for the long days and sometimes gruelling hours that made a small business very successful very quickly. I learned a great deal from her style of management:

■ *To be highly self-reliant (Emma needed me to take ownership of my job from day one)*
■ *to pay extraordinary attention to detail (between us we missed nothing)*

■ *To be very results driven ('We are here to make money' and 'The creative has to be married to the commercial' were common mantras)*

■ *To have more confidence in my work. (Although Emma was a tough boss she also piled on the praise when praise was due – which was very motivating.)"*

NICKY CONNORS

Empowering your people

When you have set up a business from scratch, it is difficult to relinquish any sort of control, particularly if you have the entrepreneurial trait of believing that you are always right! The art of delegation is a hard-won skill. However, if you find yourself constantly in demand and being asked by your staff to answer very basic questions on a regular basis, it could be that you are not empowering people to make their own decisions.

With responsibility comes experience, and the confidence to know what a good decision looks and feels like. If your team knows that you trust them, they will be willing to take more responsibility for their actions and outcomes; they will feel valued and essential members of the team. I had to learn this the hard way and had been in business for several years before I realised the extent to which delegating responsibility gives people greater motivation to do well. Finding a balance between effective delegation and maintaining control is a common challenge for many owner–managers.

Developing the ability to be an effective listener is possibly the most crucial skill a manager needs to develop.

130

Exit strategy

It was only when I decided to sell Diva that I realised the one major responsibility I had was towards my staff.

Every member of my team had shown me loyalty over the years, and to leave them without the skills or confidence to manage without me would have been the ultimate betrayal. So, whilst negotiations and due diligence were still on-going, I tasked myself to empower my team to discover that together they could do everything that I did. (In fact they already did it – but largely under my direction). I had to learn to restrain myself from answering their daily questions, but instead to reflect the question back to ask them what they would do. It worked. Gradually, the questions stopped.

I took on the service of a professional trainer in human resources, and between us we introduced a series of training days. The most successful of these was 'Understanding the team' which considered individual roles and responsibilities and then challenged each others' perceptions of what they did. The objective was to generate aware-ness and understanding of all the different roles required to make Diva successful.

Each team member began by writing down the details of their own role and responsibilities on an A4 sheet. Next, each person wrote the job description for one of their colleagues, based only on their understanding of what that person did. The two versions of the same job description were then compared. It was a revelation – and it was instantly apparent that no-one really understood what their colleagues did, or how their own role impacted on others' workload. A common problem in every company.

Next, each team member had to write down what they thought I did – and how my role interacted with each of theirs. Each descrip-tion was different, depending on what the person's role was, and how they worked with me on a daily basis. This all took place in an open discussion forum and was an eye opener for all of us in terms of how much I was involved in each area of the business.

The team was also given an assignment: to draw up a plan of action and responsibilities assuming that I was going to go on leave of absence from the business. (They didn't realise that I was leaving or that the day was part of my Exit Planning strategy.) I wanted them to realise the extent of their own knowledge and the value of the experience they had accumulated.

After an hour they had to present their results. They had jointly drawn up a highly effective plan that took account of their skills, abilities and interests and showed how they could work together very effectively and make up for my lack of presence.

From that day onwards, the team displayed confident signs of being willing and able to take greater responsibility; they also showed greater signs of understanding and respect for each others' roles. It was the best investment in people planning I could ever have made; and it left them far better able to cope when I left the business – because they knew that they could work without me.

BOOM! BUSINESS BYTES

An effective team is the most valuable asset a BOOM!ing business can have. The art of attracting, training, retaining and motivating your people may be a challenging aspect of running your company. Finding a balance between loosening the reins on your team and losing control is a hard-earned skill for any business manager.

Having the right team in place will put the BOOM! in your business.

- **The art of matching** – is an invaluable skill that will ensure you employ and work only with those people who have the professional attitude and character to match your own.
- **Be fair** – in your dealings with everyone. Introduce pay structures and contracts so that all employees are on an equal footing.
- **Encourage communication** – good ideas can come from anywhere. Listening to and involving your team will help to encourage personal initiative.
- **Empower your people** – take the time to train your team to make good decisions. It will free up your management time and may pay dividends for profitability too.
- **Use appraisals** – encourage each individual to set personal goals and develop their potential.
- **Reward initiative** – taking personal responsibility increases the ability to take informed decisions; it also allows the development of leadership potential.
- **Involve consultants** – if you use external advisors make sure they feel a part of the extended team and always pay on time.
- **Plan your exit strategy** – succession planning is part of people management. Always develop your team with tomorrow's needs in mind.

Why is customer commitment a top priority?

Always remember:

- Customers are your main business asset. Without customers you have no business.
- A successful business provides what customers want and need.
- Bad reviews travel faster and further than good ones.
- It's more expensive to attract new customers than it is to retain existing ones.

CUSTOMER COMMITMENT

YOUR CUSTOMERS ARE YOUR BUSINESS

Your business begins and ends with customer commitment. It is important to become totally tuned in to your customers' needs, because without them, you would have no business.

Do you know how others see your business? Could you describe it through your customers' eyes? Think of your company as if it were a bus. Have you ever walked on board incognito and lived every step of the customer journey as though you were travelling as a passenger?

The secret of customer commitment is not only to be an expert in your field (Business Discipline No.3) but also to become an expert in your customers' buying patterns: to know how they think, what they want, what will trigger them to buy from you and what may turn them away. Business Discipline No.6 will add to your understanding of the customer experience and will help you to focus on making your customers feel so good they will never have a reason to defect to the competition.

Know what makes your company unique

Customer commitment works hand in hand with new business development and marketing. It represents your company's values and standards of delivery, but is also a valuable route to business growth. Make sure that you know enough about the style and ethos of your competitors (Business Discipline No.3) to be clear about points of differentiation, such as price levels, quality, aftercare, business ethos, quality of surroundings, green credentials and so on.

See your business through your customers' eyes.

Ask yourself and your team:
■ What additional things could you introduce into your service to improve your customers' experience to create a positive and lasting impression?

More like planning a formal dinner than organising a casual barbecue, the basic fundamentals of BOOM!ing customer satisfaction are: efficient forward planning (anticipating your customers' requirements), exceptional manners (making them feel they are unique), being a perfect host (looking after their needs), providing a positive and unique experience to remember (your goods or service) and quality follow-up after the event (making sure they enjoyed the experience). The ideal outcome is for your customer to feel as if they have received *more than* value for money, at no extra cost to you.

The more memorable you can be – for positive reasons – the more likely your customers are to return.

Customer commitment need cost your company very little or nothing at all and should give you everything back in return. You should be able to answer the following questions:

■ What is it about your business that leads customers to choose your products or service?
■ What has caused customers to turn away in the past?
■ What can you do to improve customer commitment and attract more of the right kind of customers?
■ Are you offering the best levels of customer care possible?

Customers are a business asset. Without them your business would not survive.

Who are your customers?

It may seem an obvious question, but who *are* your customers? (What do they do? How do they think? What are their values? Why do they need you? What do they want?) Do you know which of your customers currently contribute most to your annual revenue? It's a cliché but it is usually true that 80 per cent of your income will be coming from 20 per cent of your customers.

Every small business enterprise begins with a great idea or opportunity. That idea is based on a mixture of commercial and/ or personal experience and *a lot* of assumptions about who your customers are, what they need, and what they will pay for your products or services. Some of those assumptions will be right – and some of them may need to be revised once you know more about your market. All assumptions need to be tested, and regularly.

Once you have analysed your own business' results and have assessed which of your clients represent your top 20 per cent, you are able to ask:

Who are my customers?

■ What do I know about my customers and how can I learn more about their buying behaviour?

■ What did the top 20 per cent buy and why did they buy it?

■ How can I increase revenue further from the top 20 per cent?

■ Which of those making up the 80 per cent would I like to do more business with and which are potentially high-value clients?

Keep reviewing your customers' wants and needs.

Be very careful not to make too many assumptions about who your customers are and what they want. A mature business may know and be able to rely upon one set of customers – but may become vulnerable if something happens that they can't control (retail outlets in a small town lose custom when a large local employer closes; service industries suffer when it is cheaper to outsource labour overseas). Knowing what those customers value about your company and gathering testimonials on an on-going basis will leave you in a good position to approach new clients when you can see change coming.

Do you know where your customers came from?

- How many new customers did you get via referral?
- How many were personal recommendations?
- How many are repeat business?

Undertaking a complete review of your customers can become a time-consuming task if you do it retrospectively. It is well worth devising a simple system of categorisation, probably on an Excel spreadsheet or similar, to capture your customers' basic details when you first do business with them.

The 80/20 rule

Expanding a business does not always require further staff or resources; there just needs to be greater clarity concerning where the money is coming from. The 80/20 rule works every time.

"At the time I approached Emma for guidance I felt as if I was at full capacity in terms of the workload I was carrying. I was considering taking on a trainee graduate to help me to bring in new business. Emma helped me to reframe my plans. Her first question was, 'Do you know where the majority of your revenue is coming from? Which of your customers are making you money?'

In truth, I didn't know. Her advice was to first analyse my annual return by customer and by type of customer. So I did as she suggested, and I was amazed. The 80/20 rule really does hold true. Twenty per cent of my customers were delivering 80 per cent of my income.

'Give everything, except the top category clients – to your assistant,' she said. 'You know she is reliable and you know she does excellent work. You've got to do that if you want to grow. It will free you up to develop new business. Otherwise you'll be so busy trying to give a perfect service to everyone personally that all your clients will suffer and you won't grow the business at all.'

So that's pretty much what I've done, and we've expanded as a result. I now spend more time face to face with customers, learning what makes them tick. I know and understand them better and I feel closer to their business needs.

When you first start a business there is a great temptation to say 'yes' to any business for anybody for very little reward. And you do that because you want to get your name out there; you want to build a reputation. Any money coming through the door seems better than none. But being more discerning about what we will and won't take on is leading to an increase in higher ticket business, which is in itself more rewarding.**"**   **PETER READ, READ INSURANCE**

What do your customers want?

On one level what customers want is generally very simple: they want you to deliver what you promised, on time and to budget, they want to be kept informed if anything has gone wrong that will affect quality or delivery; and they want a consistent quality of goods or service.

But actually what they also want is to experience the BOOM! factor: the full-on impact of those BOOM!preneur qualities of passion, attitude and honesty. They want to feel as if they are the best and only customer you have; to feel appreciated, under-stood, welcomed back; they would like you to manage their expectations so effectively that they sense they are getting more than they wished for; they would like to feel a personal rapport and to know that you understand their every need. They want to buy the qualities that you and your brand represent.

Personal qualities add the BOOM! factor to customer relationships and keep them coming back for more.

As with each of the BOOM! disciplines, you should always REVIEW, your current customer strategy before you PLAN your next steps and DO what you need to do to win new business.

How can you know your customers better?

The first meeting with a new client is like the first stage of any new relationship. All parties are trying to present at their best and to impress one another. It is a very useful time to find out about longer-term plans and aspirations; what is working for them and what is not – in the context of the goods or services you may be able to provide in future.

Always ask your customers plenty of questions. Ask them what their expectations are from your company, what they are pleased with and not so pleased with in regard to previous experiences. Get to know as much about them as possible from the outset.

Remember that the process of 'matching' (page 121) applies not only to those you work with but to your customers too. Hopefully you and your customer will be a perfect fit of needs and expectations, but not all business dealings run that smoothly:

■ If you are going to be spending any length of time with your customer and you feel you are incompatible in a major way, then be honest and step away – before a contract is signed.
■ If what the customer is asking for falls outside what your business can deliver, tell them – they will appreciate your honesty and will be able to make other plans.
■ If you feel something is 'wrong' midway through a contract, you

are probably right. Ask direct questions. Find out your customers' concerns so that you can address them. If you ignore your instincts, the situation will certainly deteriorate.

How your customers can help you

Satisfied customers are (usually) happy customers and it is human nature to want to give back to those who have helped us, to say thank you, or to make recommendations – but customers need to be shown how to do so. You can help your customers to help you to get to know them better by:

- Giving them non-financial benefits or a reward system
- Encouraging them to provide you with testimonials
- Providing them with an easy-to-complete questionnaire that provides candid feedback about your services and suggestions
- Asking them to recommend you to others – and offering incentives to do so
- Gathering information that can be used via different media for marketing purposes

Customer care and marketing are partners in business. One can help the other. Good customer care generates quality data (names, addresses, buying habits) that can be converted into sales via a marketing campaign. Likewise, a supporting marketing campaign can generate more customers who can provide more information – and so it goes on. The strategies to achieve this will differ according to the needs of your specific industry (see Business Discipline No.3).

! Do remember that there are strict legal guidelines on the gathering, usage and storage of third party information. If you are creating a customer database, you will need to comply with the terms of use outlined in the Data Protection Act 1998. See Further Resources.

Stay true to your strategy

Think of a typical customer service department and you may think of people whose main role is to field questions, soothe tempers, solve problems and issue refunds. They perform a very important function, but that function is very reactive. They are providing customer care – often to customers who have a complaint or a problem – with a view to protecting the company and safe-guarding reputation.

Customer commitment includes awareness of customer care and is always about customer service; but in the world of the BOOM!preneur it involves anticipating what your customers will need before they realise it themselves and providing what they desire before they have to ask – because you will already have found out what they want.

It is not about serving customers at the expense of your profit (although occasionally it may be), or trying to be all things to all people; it doesn't mean changing the direction of your business strategy every time another customer walks through your door. That way chaos lies! It is always a planned and proactive response. It is about staying true to your Business Strategy (Business Discipline No.1) and your Business Plan (Business Discipline No.2) but being flexible enough to adapt within those parameters to give your customers what they want – while constantly seeking feedback from your customers to ensure that you are taking the right approach.

Remember that you and your values are part of what your customer is buying. When they buy they are also buying what you represent – and that means your expertise. As the owner of Diva I positioned myself as the expert in my business niche. I was very honest. I made sure that my customers understood the process that they were getting involved in as well as the end product that they were buying.

Deliver on your promises

This is the paragraph that cracks the whip and reminds you that customer commitment is a *discipline*. It is not an occasional or optional activity; it is an integral part of everything you do in your day to day business.

The only way you can make a customer truly happy is to deliver on your promises. That is the message that you have to instil in everyone in your company.

When you have a wonderful meal at a restaurant you want to be confident that when you return, you will repeat that enjoyable experience. All customers want consistency of quality and approach. No-one wants to change suppliers unless they have to; it is time consuming and inconvenient.

Remember:

■ It's more expensive to attract new customers than it is to retain existing ones

■ If your product or service doesn't deliver, your customers will go elsewhere

■ An unhappy customer will tell nine friends. A happy customer may only tell one

■ Be consistent in your approach and loyalties

Set the example

First impressions are lasting impressions. If you want to give a positive impression, you need to ensure that your values are being transmitted throughout your company, at every level – as well as via marketing and PR material and via your website.

The larger your team, and the more spread out you are within the office, the harder it can be to ensure consistency of approach. Make sure that your values are very clearly understood by everyone at every level. If your company is large enough to support a receptionist, remember, he or she will speak to and see many

All customers should feel they are your only customer at the point of delivery.

more people who contact the business than you do. It is an important outward-facing role that will influence any meeting or action that follows. A short induction programme and standard guidelines for customer care can be a useful way to ensure every-one understands what is required.

- Is everyone within the company aware of your expectations?
- Does everyone have the same production/delivery schedule so that information given to customers is consistent?
- Does everyone know what is appropriate and what is not in terms of courtesy, sharing information and behaviour towards your clients?
- Does everyone answer the phone in a consistently polite manner? Some people may need to be briefed on how to field calls professionally and appropriately.
- Do you consistently follow up with customers to see whether their experience was positive?

Contented customers will return and will recommend you to others; they add value to the volume of your sales and to the value of your business. Finding ways to enhance customer service will always make a positive difference regardless of the business or industry you are in.

Relationships matter

Customer commitment is of equal importance whether you are running a service-driven company or selling goods in the retail sector. Income makes your business profitable but the quality of your business relationships determines lasting success.

Most people learn quickly that it is important to engage with customers, be enthusiastic, and make sure they know you are willing to go the extra mile to deliver results. Reliability, professionalism, consistency, enthusiasm for the task in hand and effective communication are essential skills that show customers you care.

In running EMpwr, my mentoring company, I am often struck by both the similarities and the differences between running a retail business and offering a business service. The commercial priorities are the same: financial management and forward planning are daily essentials, but the core difference is that when you run a service company you become the product.

Whereas my Diva customers measured my commitment according to unit cost, profit margin, speed and quality of delivery; as a business mentor I am assessed according to more value-driven criteria. My clients are not buying a manufactured product; they want my business knowledge and experience. The commercial exchange is more personal than material. Quality and reliability remain very important but cost is rarely the over-riding concern. Instead clients rely on tangible evidence that they are receiving sound advice and value for money. We also need to have a working rapport. There has to be a 'feel good' factor and there often a partial sense of ownership on their part too. Which of us doesn't refer to 'my' solicitor, 'my' dentist, 'my' hairdresser but 'the' supermarket, 'the' chemist? In a service industry the relationship with the customer is all important.

It is worth remembering that colleagues and associates are also your customers. You need to commit to building positive relationships with them in the same way as you would a new client. If you show appreciation to the warehouse manager you are more likely to get fast-track service when occasion demands it. If you treat the receptionist with courtesy and brief him or her about key clients then you and your clients will benefit too. Relationships always matter.

BOOM! BUSINESS BYTES

An effective BOOM!preneur knows what their customer wants before they know it themselves, though sometimes their needs have to be balanced against the aims you set out in your business strategy.

Always give your customers a good reason to return – because without customers you have no business.

- **Get to know your customers** – they are your lifeblood and you need to understand their buying triggers: what they want, what they need, and what benefits your business can offer them.

- **Look after the top 20 per cent** – the 80/20 rule usually applies to customers. Eighty per cent of your revenue will be coming from 20 per cent of your customers.

- **Review the revenue** – find out who is making your business money; who is losing you money – in non-payment or late payments or by being overly demanding; and who is useful in terms of contacts and recommendations.

- **Plan to expand** – rather than spread yourself thinly, focus on developing your core customer base – but remain aware of other avenues of development.

- **Watch the competition** – one business owner's loss is another business owner's gain. Keep an eye on your competitors and plan to stay ahead of the game – by always giving your customers more than they knew they wanted – at no extra expense to you.

- **Be consistent in approach** – if you find you are unable to deliver consistently good service to all your customers, your business will suffer.

- **Help your customers to help you** – ask them for feedback and give equal credence to complaints and compliments.

What has personal development to do with business?

Personal development is important because you *are* your business:

- Pay attention to your own needs.
- It doesn't have to be lonely at the top.
- Find ways to maintain your personal momentum.
- Be passionate about all aspects of your life and business.

PERSONAL DEVELOPMENT

MOTIVATE YOURSELF

Personal development is the final BOOM! Business Discipline and is the one that may determine your ultimate success. The success of every business begins and ends with the attitude and drive of the person at the top.

All business success begins with high energy and enthusiasm driven by personal motivation and a willingness to learn, develop and change. Business growth depends upon it. Unless you feel fully committed, care about what you are doing and have the energy to run the company, your business journey is likely to become an uphill struggle.

Your needs are the same as the needs of your business

When I was managing director of Diva Cosmetics, it is probably true to say that my own personal development was the least of my business priorities. This is not an unusual scenario and is one that I see frequently in my role as a business mentor. Focused intently on nurturing clients and customers, looking out for the welfare of staff, worried in some instances about childcare and home arrangements, there are few business owners who feel able to put their own needs ahead of their business or family.

And yet you and your business are an extension of each other. You would not neglect any other aspect of business development – so it is important that you do not neglect your own development either. Owner–managers need always to remember that, yes, they're running a business, but they need to keep the rest of their life in order as well because that can impact on business outcomes.

It is not unusual for business leaders to feel isolated with their issues, concerned that they have lost their way or are losing personal motivation. Many do not have the work–life balance that they would prefer and may start to question why they chose such a challenging path.

The old saying is a true saying – keep doing what you are doing, and you will keep getting what you've got.

A management accountant once told me that he worries when he sees that a business owner has let him- or herself go physically. He sees the physical state as indicative of the mental state. Too often he says, it is an indication that the business is in trouble.

Now I'm not trying to tell you to keep fit, go on a diet or to make any other health or lifestyle-related choices. What I will say is that if you can tell that your levels of motivation have dropped, it really is up to you to bring about a change and do something about it. One of the biggest challenges in business is to find ways to maintain your own motivation. If you lose your way, your team and your customers will eventually recognise it; it will impact on the future of your business. This really is a very important point.

When life feels awful we tend to be motivated to bring about change. A lot of business mentoring begins at a point of business crisis – or at a mid-point where the process of change has already begun. It gives me the greatest sense of work satisfaction when a client tells me at the end of a session that they are feeling re-energised, fired up and raring to go. That's exactly what your personal development needs to deliver to you.

Plan for personal development

Personal growth comes about only if you are aware that it is necessary. Many people who are unhappy with aspects of their business life are slow to realise that they will need to change something that is familiar in order to transform discomfort into personal happiness and fulfilment.

Personal development means taking a strategic and practical approach to assessing your own needs – for your benefit, and for that of your business; but first it is essential to determine exactly areas which need development.

Personal development requires as much dedication and focus as the other Business Disciplines but needn't be time-consuming or difficult. Sometimes the simplest change can bring about the greatest transformation. Focus on your end goal and what it would mean to you to achieve it.

The myth of work–life balance

I discovered the hard way that everyone needs to find their own definition of what work–life balance is and what mix works for them and their family. After all, your work is part of your life, so how can you create an artificial boundary between the two?

There are books and magazine articles aplenty that espouse the secrets of 'having a ball and having it all' – which just goes to show what we all aspire to. Unless your company is large and established enough for you to be able to rely on experienced staff, or pay others to take a great deal of the strain, there is rarely any such thing as 'having it all' in work and in play. Something, somewhere, has to give. Many of you will know the sense of guilt that comes with having to explain to your girlfriend, boyfriend, spouse or friends why work appears to be your most important priority. There are an awful lot of successful entrepreneurs who know only too well that they missed out on precious moments of their children's childhood. Those are choices that we all have to make. You are the only one who can decide what kind of balance you want, and what kind of lifestyle will work for you.

In reality, if your life seems to be dominated by work and you feel you are missing out on other priorities in life, there is often a practical solution.

WHAT'S THE INCENTIVE?
Are you really committed to your own development? When deciding on your personal priorities, ask yourself how desirable the outcome will be on a scale of 1–10. Only those that score a high 10 are likely to be achieved.

152

Life is a balancing act

Barbara Cox, CEO of Nutrichef, is the first to admit that home–work balance has been one of her greatest personal challenges. It was one of her triggers for contacting me as a business mentor. She felt sure that she could be achieving more by making different choices and adapting her use of time – and she was right:

*"*I have two delightful children: a 12-year-old and an 8-year-old, and my youngest was just 3 years old when I first started Nutrichef. One of my greatest areas of guilt was that I wasn't spending enough time with them and was never involved in the school-run, I was forever putting work ahead of my home commitments. Typical of many business-owners, I felt that I had to sign off on every business decision. I decided that I needed a business mentor precisely because I was unsure how best to delegate and I was concerned about how I would cope as the business continued to grow.

There has been a very positive outcome. I have gradually learned to delegate in a masterful fashion – which in turn has empowered my team to take more responsibility and have a greater sense of owner-ship. I've also learnt that you really *can* have a day off once in a while. It's just a matter of getting everything prepared in advance. Work from home, use your Blackberry more, learn to delegate; know that it is okay, you *can* let go a little bit but still keep control of the reins.

And importantly, I am paying much greater attention to the personal 'match' of those I hire. I have learned that it is very important to recruit those whose personal qualities you can rely upon: a 'mini me' if you like.*"*

BARBARA COX

I visualise work–life balance to be like an old-fashioned set of scales: by adding, removing or moving priorities like weights on each scale, you can eventually achieve perfect balance. But the scales will also tip dramatically to either the right or to the left if you overload either side – and the balance is lost. Where this tipping point lies in real life depends on how guilty you feel. The guilt is what tips the balance. Managing guilt is an important element of becoming successful. Any professional athlete will tell you that in order to be the best they frequently had to put their own needs ahead of others'. Business owners make similar choices.

The other important element is self-discipline. If you really, really want to redress the balance you will schedule realistic times in which to do things – and do everything it takes to keep those commitments. You deserve to create the kind of life that you want and no one is going to stand in your way except for you.

It really is lonely at the top

It's a well-worn cliché but an awful lot of people discover over the years that it really is lonely at the top – and it's even lonelier if you are a sole trader with only yourself for company each day. Running a business may be the loneliest thing you'll ever do.

"I consider having a mentor to be a crucial part of my 'me' time. I don't think of the time spent as being solely work-orientated because I don't think you can separate the personal when you are running a business. Essentially, when you are running your own business, you are the business."

SARAH ISAACS, MD, KITELEYS SOLICITORS

A business mentor can be an excellent antidote to moments of leadership wobble: times when frustration with suppliers, staff or the state of your industry can temporarily 'lower the boom' and take the wind out of your sails. Of course, I am a mentor, so I would say that wouldn't I? However, I know from experience that it is unfair to involve your family or friends in business dilemmas and strategic quandaries because their instincts will be to protect you and the household from unnecessary stress or risk.

154

A mentor or other business advisor on the other hand can say, 'You're making the right decision for this business – and now you need to adjust your Business Plan to support your strategy.'

Priorities for personal development

Every business person has different priorities for personal development. They may relate to your work, leisure activities, personal or family time, but it is important to know what they are.

You may need to take stock to understand your work style and practices. For example, most people find that they have peak times of day when they are at their most productive. I am very much a morning person. Organisation and self-discipline are extremely important to me and I like to feel that the majority of my work is done by the time my children are home from school. However, you will also find me at my desk late at night when necessary.

Many self-employed people find it hard to know where to draw the line in their working day, especially if they work from home. There is only one answer: plan ahead, manage your time and focus on developing the self-discipline to start and end at set times each day. Close the office door at the end of the working day and make sure you commit yourself to doing other things in the evening to force a change of pace. The lessons to take away from this are really quite simple:

■ Don't forget your own needs and your family's needs.
■ Respect your own health and well-being and schedule ample time during the working week to do things that will re-ignite your passion and motivation for your business.

"I think everyone in business needs a mentor. I really, really do. It can be a lonely old place up here. Whether it's just to bounce ideas, whether it's staff issues, or personal issues, just to speak to someone else who's been there, done that, understands where you're coming from and just to know that you're on the right track – objective advice really."

BARBARA COX, *CEO, NUTRICHEF*

- Be true to yourself and don't feel obliged to aspire to someone else's idea of what a perfectly balanced life looks like.
- Invest in your own professional development for your own benefit as well as that of your business.

Take your personal development as seriously as any other aspect of your business. Schedule time for training, days off, an annual holiday, staff 'away days' or events. The reality is that the happier you are in your work and the better organised you are the more it will show in your demeanour, your tone of voice, your management style and your energy levels. If you are happy in your work, the likelihood is that your team will be contented too.

Tipping points

My own priority for personal development has always been to find a way of combining my passion for business with the needs of my growing family and it hasn't always been easy!

I had only just set up Diva Cosmetics when my first son was born, and I felt I had no choice but to keep on working. At only 8 weeks old William was attending an excellent nursery for four days a week – from 8am until 6pm. Other mothers may judge me for it, but I don't believe that William had a compromised early childhood – quite the reverse. He spent his days surrounded by other children, who have since become proper friends; learnt to share and to tolerate others; and he was cared for in a stimulating environment, discovering the joys of finger painting, mud pies and 'cooking'. I was able to ensure that Fridays, Saturdays and Sundays were 'William and me time' when I tried not to be distracted by work ... honestly I did! I knew that I didn't have the perfect work–life balance but I was doing everything possible to try and achieve it. However, life and circumstances change.

My first work–parenting 'tipping point' occurred one beautiful day in April 2002. The sun was shining, the sky was bright blue and I was having lunch with a supplier at a beach-side restaurant, in Bournemouth. During lunch I looked out of the window and noticed that the beach was full of mums with their children playing in the weekday sunshine; and I thought to myself, 'I'll never do that with William.' I felt a profound sense of loss and an awareness of the passing of time that still hits me when I think of it now. I took a vow at that moment that if I ever had more children I would not work. I would spend my time with them. It was a sincere vow – and I always fulfil my promises.

I couldn't deliver on my promise immediately because I had a business to run and people were reliant on me: suppliers, customers, my team. There was no way I could just go home and walk away at that moment in time. But the moment of realisation stayed with me and I began to plan my exit strategy from Diva.

I sold my company eighteen months later, soon after I became pregnant with my second child, Charlie. My daughter Hattie was born the following year and I was all set to become the perfect stay-at-home mum. But as much as I love my children dearly I didn't really enjoy being at home all day and I began to dread the weekdays. The people who told me, when I sold Diva, that I wouldn't enjoy being at home, clearly knew me better than I knew myself. It took quite a while to admit how I was feeling and to realise that I missed working. I missed the buzz of an opportunity – of closing a deal, of making a profit, and of being with other adults. It took even longer to realise that to feel this way didn't make me a bad parent. It actually showed me that each of us is different, with a different definition of what success means for us as individuals, and with different needs in life.

At the time I sold Diva, my entire sense of purpose revolved around being a full-time mum. It works for many people; it didn't work for me. I now know that my life will always include my work. I love running my business – and when I am happy, my family is happy and my home runs more smoothly. I am not someone who *should* be a stay-at-home mum – but I had to try it out to know.

In order to be happy in life, you must first accept and like yourself for who you are.

Nor is my state of satisfaction likely to remain constant. There will be further tipping points for change in the future. I know that I will always struggle to be a domestic goddess.

BOOM! BUSINESS BYTES

Making time for your own personal development can be a challenge when commercial considerations seem more pressing; but it is important to have other things in your life to balance your focus on work and business. The rewards will be personal as well as financial; the benefits will be for others as well as you. The professionals that you need to consult, concerning whether you've got the balance right, are those who know you best – your friends and family.

- **You are the future of your business** – so look after yourself with the same degree of care than you would maintain your customers.
- **Pay attention** – be aware of your levels of productivity. If you are achieving less than you could and you are losing your sense of joy in your work – then it's either time for a holiday or time to change the way you are working.
- **Stay healthy** – your health is important – to your staff, your family and your livelihood.
- **Keep in touch** – with other people in your industry, with friends, former colleagues and customers. It can be lonely at the top – but only if you isolate yourself. You can share ideas and solutions to problems without giving away your company secrets.
- **Stay open-minded** – only you can know what truly works for you. To parents who are struggling to juggle parenthood with the needs of their work, I say make no assumptions about your ideal work–life balance until you've tried different ways of living. Discover your own ideal – taking into consideration time and finances.

We are all individuals – and BOOM!preneurs are more individual than most!

PART THREE

THE BOOM! BUSINESS TOOLBOX

9 principles of planning

Business Discipline No.2 explained the importance of creating and using a comprehensive Business Plan. This section explains the key purpose and benefits of the nine sections of a typical Business Plan and how to prepare one as a starting point for review:

Section 1   Business overview
Section 2   Operational overview
Section 3   Industry overview
Section 4   Marketing overview
Section 5   Financial forecasts
Section 6   Management and staffing
Section 7   Regulatory issues
Section 8   Considerations
Section 9   Executive summary

THE PRINCIPLES OF BUSINESS PLANNING

Section one: Business overview

Purpose

■ To provide an overview of your business, including your aims and vision for the future, summarising where you started, where you are now, and where you are aiming to get to – usually within a defined time-frame.

Benefit

■ Provides an accurate and focused starting point for review.

What to include

■ **History** – A definition of your industry sector, your place within it and a short history of your company. Explain whether you bought the company or started from scratch.

■ **Vision** – Your strategic statement (from Business Discipline No.1) and your vision for the future.

■ **Objectives** – Your aims when you started trading and whether you are still on track and in tune with those aims.

■ **Ownership** – The structure and type of business – whether you are a sole trader, limited company or PLC.

Make sure this section is honest, accurate, concise and realistic.

Business overview

History

Vision

Objectives

Ownership

Section one: Business overview

Your Business Plan should be referred to regularly: weekly, monthly and throughout the year.

Section two: Operational overview – products and services

Purpose

■ To provide a clear description of the purpose of your business: what it offers and what it does not; what it plans to offer in the future.

Benefit

■ Shows the main focus of your business and the unique factors that differentiate your offering from that of your competitors.

What to include

■ **Description of products and services** – What you do, what you produce, what you offer – and why it is unique.

■ **Key features and benefits** – Any rights to products, trademarks, patents or properties. Your pricing strategy and whether it is consistent with your quality of product, service and in line with the market expectation.

■ **Plans for product development** – What plans you have to develop your range of products or services.

■ **Competitive advantages** – Why you are best placed to provide the product or service. What differentiates your business from the competition. Who your customers are and what they can expect from you. Why your customers would return to your company or recommend you to others.

Section two of your plan also needs to take account of the operational side of your business and how you will deliver your products or services.

Products and services

Description of products or services	Key features
Plans for future products and services	Competitive advantages

Section two: Products and services

Clarity of purpose enables your customers to understand what to expect from your company.

Section two: Operational overview – business processes

Purpose

- To provide a clear description of the way your business functions, any unique production features or processes and what you plan to offer in the future. Make sure that your description is easy to understand and jargon-free.

Benefit

- Offers a starting point for reviewing production capacity, assessing future plant cost requirements and monitoring the speed of technological change.

What to include

- **The production process** – Summarise your production process; whether you produce everything you need yourself, whether you outsource, and the cost of outsourcing.
- **Supply chain analysis** – Which sources of supply are cheapest and whether you need to source supplies from elsewhere; your strategy for research. Assessment of investment needed and over what timescale. Include mention of any technological changes in the industry.
- **Property and machinery** – List any property that you lease or own and the financial commitment associated with it. Note whether you have any plans to change your situation.

Operational review

Production process	■ Summarise the process for your particular products or services
Supply chain analysis	■ Identify key suppliers and £ spent per year – noting percentage of total spend ■ Identify cost and timing implications of outsourcing
Property or machinery	■ Identify property and machinery that you lease or own – including financial commitments ■ Identify future investment needs

Section two: Operational review

Smooth delivery is an essential aspect of planning ahead.

Section three: Industry overview

Purpose

■ To demonstrate enough knowledge to be an expert in your industry sector with a clear idea of your place and role within it. Include a summary of key market trends and their potential impact on your business.

Benefit

■ Demonstrates that you are an expert in your field, that you are aware of how the 'big picture' can impact on the content, process, location or function of your business; and that it is important to adapt in anticipation, not in retrospect.

What to include

■ **Industry size** – The size and scope of your market sector by value and volume. How many companies are making how much money? Which sector are you in? How has it changed size since last year? What are the prospects for growth?

■ **Market breakdown** – Break down the sub-sections within your sector and compare growth trends and value. Include an overview of your primary customers.

■ **Key market trends** – Where are the increases and the decline in demand? What are the future trends in the industry? What technological changes are likely to impact on your business?

■ **Market outlook** – How does your business need to adapt to survive and grow in the future?

■ **Key changes in the last twelve months** – Which major players have changed ownership, changed suppliers, changed management – and what impact will that have on your business?

■ **Competitive review** – A brief overview of your competitors. Ask yourself, Who am I competing with? What are my competitors doing? How do I compare? Assess your future strategy.

Industry overview

Overall size of industry

Key product and market segments

Key market trends

Outlook for your market

Key changes in the last 12 months

Competitive review

Section three: Industry overview

All areas of the world have been affected by the technological revolution of the past thirty years – and it is continuing to reshape jobs, markets, pricing policies and trends in international trade. Taking the time to review the current state of your industry and your place within it is absolutely crucial to business survival.

Every industry is subject to change. It is important to stay tuned in to what's going on at a legislative level.

Section four: Marketing overview

Purpose

■ To encourage you to stay aware of what is going on in your industry.

■ To provide a detailed overview of the marketplace.

■ To identify who will buy your products or services and how best to supply their needs.

Benefit

■ With a sharply defined customer profile and clear understanding of who your customers are and what they want, it becomes easier to quantify and allocate marketing spend that will deliver productive outcomes.

What to include

■ **Your target market** – Who you are aiming at with your business? What is the demographic profile? How big is your target market? What are the forward trends?

■ **Customer buying process and criteria** – Get into the mindset of your customers. What buying decisions do they make? What do they want? What do they need? How often do they need it? How much are they willing to pay? What are you doing to get them to buy?

■ **Review of your market position** – Where do you sit in your market? Understand your point of differentiation. Remain aware of market changes. Include a note of your distribution channels.

■ **Pricing overview** – Be aware of your pricing in relation to your competitors'.

■ **Marketing tactics** – Stay sharp in relation to your competitors' strategies. Are they advertising successfully? What is their marketing budget? What level of activity are they committing to – and what are you planning to do about it?

172

Marketing overview

Target market

Customer buying process and criteria

Review of your position in the marketplace vs. competition

Pricing overview vs. competition

Marketing tactics

Section four: Marketing overview

The marketing overview requires market research to do it well. The overview works in partnership with Business Discipline No.3 and is a portrait of your place in the market in relation to your market strategy. It will profile your core customers and what they want from your products or services in order to better understand how they make buying decisions.

Your marketing overview will define your marketing budget for the year.

Section five: Financial forecasts

Purpose

■ To review your business from a financial point of view and forecast as accurately as possible the earnings and expenditure over the course of a defined time period.

■ To identify levels of working capital and expected net profit, and adjust sales and marketing strategy accordingly.

Benefit

■ Provides the big financial picture which impacts on every area of the business from staff appointments to stockholding. Ignore this section at your company's peril.

What to include

■ **Sales forecasts** – A projection of sales on a daily, weekly or monthly basis, broken down into specific categories by product and by customer.

■ **Cashflow forecasts** – Daily, weekly or monthly forecasts that provide an assessment of current income and scheduled outgoings. They allow you to spot problems before they happen.

■ **Your profit and loss forecast** – Showing operating profit and net return; it can be provided by your accountant.

■ **Balance sheet** – A financial summary that sums up your company's finances and includes all assets and liabilities.

The intention in your financial forecast is to show whether you have enough working capital to function throughout the year; to what extent you will be making a profit after your costs and over-heads have been taken into account; and whether the money you expect to raise from sales or services is sufficient and in line with your strategic aims. Typically forecasts are projected over three or five years, but every business should have a detailed twelve-month plan.

Financial forecasts

Sales forecasts

Prepare a daily/weekly/monthly forecast of your sales

Why?
■ Essential to monitor income in order to cover costs

Break down income into key areas to provide necessary information. For example:
■ By product
■ By customer

Why?
■ Essential to monitor sales versus forecasts in order to assess stock requirements.
■ Monitoring by customer will enable you to see if sales are as expected – to guide sales focus and sales strategy.

Cashflow

Prepare a daily/weekly/monthly forecast of all your outgoings. Include all costs. (Include your VAT repayments if you are VAT registered.)

Why?
■ You need to ensure that you have sufficient funds to cover your costs. This detailed forecast will enable you to anticipate problems and plan around them. For example, by instigating a sales drive to increase income.

Break down your costs into key areas. For example:
■ Staffing costs
■ Supply costs
■ Overheads

Why?
■ Enables you to see at a glance how much each area of the business is costing.

Section five: Financial forecasts

Financial control is at the heart of business success.

Section six: Management and staffing

Purpose

■   To provide an overview of the present and future function and cost of personnel with reporting structure and an assessment of productivity and training requirements. Include costs and timescales for all aspects of your plan.

Benefit

■   Allows present and future skills and capability to be factored fully into any plans for changes in workload, skills requirement, business development and future growth.

What to include

■   **Organisational structure** – How your company is organised. Strengths and weaknesses. Future developments. Company salary scale and benefits package.

■   **Management team** – The size of the management team, their CVs, job descriptions, levels of accountability. Strengths and weaknesses. Any litigious matters.

■   **Current staff** – The number of people employed in each department, their roles and what they earn. Contribution per employee in financial terms if appropriate. Employee retention rates. Strengths and weaknesses. Any disciplinary issues.

■   **Future staffing requirements** – Your plans for recruitment and any investment necessary for new appointments. The number of people you use on a freelance basis and how much they cost you per project and per annum. Budget per head.

■   **Training and development** – Assessment of skills shortages and likely investment in training. Plans to motivate and train staff. Budget per head.

176

Management and staffing

Organisational structure

Management team

Current staff

Future staffing requirements

Training and development

Section six: Management and staffing

Your people are an essential business resource. Each member of staff represents an investment and hopefully a return on that investment (either directly or indirectly). The level of detail that is included in your Business Plan will depend upon the speed and scope of your business growth and whether you are looking for external finance. Include an overview of job title, primary business skills, salary, and potential return for each staff member.

Your people are your future. Each role within the company should be clearly defined.

Section seven: Regulatory issues

Purpose

- To remain aware that non-compliance in regulatory matters can be a major threat to profitability.
- To remain aware of contractual commitments.
- To assess the value of intellectual property and its impact on new product development.

Benefit

- Primarily an overview of the financial value of any intellectual property and its strategic value.

What to include

- **Patents, trademarks, licenses, estates** – Intellectual property rights owned or licensed by the company. The financial value of intellectual property. Special issues.
- **Contracts, licenses and terms of business** – Numbers of contracts, special terms, and financial value. Strategy for future development if there are no standards in place.
- **Regulations** – A note of any regulatory issues that impact on your production or service. Future changes and any associated costs involved.
- **Health and safety** – Any costs likely to be involved in ensuring conformity to guidelines.

Every industry sector has regulatory guidelines and it is your responsibility to remain aware of what they are and what is required to ensure that your products or services are safe, secure and legally watertight. Mistakes can be costly, especially if you find yourself in contravention of any health and safety guidelines, patent guidelines, copyright considerations or trading laws.

Regulatory issues

Patents, trademarks, licenses, estates	Contracts
Regulations	Health and safety

Section seven: Regulatory issues

Never underestimate the importance of legal compliance and always factor in the cost of safety checks.

Section eight: Considerations

Purpose

■ To provide an overview of current and potential threats to your business together with cost implications. The simplest form of risk assessment is via a 'SWOT' analysis (a review of 'Strengths, Weaknesses, Opportunities and Threats'). Allow financial contingency for risks not covered by commercial insurance.

Benefit

■ Will ensure that you remain alert to the risk factors in your business and that unnecessary risks are mitigated through efficient planning and by process of due diligence.

What to include

Every business owner takes risks, it comes with the job; but there are several areas that need conscious assessment as part of your Business Plan:

■ **Market risk** – Changes in the marketplace or a threat from a competitor.

■ **Personal risk** – To your livelihood, your business or your home through litigation or commercial crises.

■ **Financial risk** – Problems with cashflow and late payment remain the primary causes of business failure.

■ **Operational risk** – Are your IT equipment, your premises and your suppliers' production capabilities secure, up to date and free from risk of theft or breakdown? Are your staff well-trained, loyal and productive?

■ **Other risks** – Importing goods and materials may carry a risk if there is political or economic instability in the country concerned. Fluctuating exchange rates can have a major impact on the cost of raw materials and the price of production.

Considerations

Section eight: Considerations

! Remember: you have a legal obligation to ensure that your work-place is safe for your employees and free of hazards. If in any doubt, contact the Health and Safety Executive.

An annual risk assessment can save your business time, money and legal costs.

Section nine: Executive summary

Purpose

■ A summary of everything that is covered in your Business Plan, it will include the strategic statement that you devised in Business Discipline No.1. It will also provide an overview of the key points from rest of the document.

Benefit

■ Provides an 'at a view' snapshot of the current business that is the starting point for each business review.

■ A summary for third-party investors.

What to include

■ Business description
■ Ownership and management
■ Strategic statement (50 words)
■ Marketing opportunities
■ Competitive advantages
■ Summary of financial projections

This should appear as the first page of your Business Plan but is usually completed last as it draws together information from each of the other sections. This page sums up what your business is about and is the one section that you can guarantee potential investors and others will assess before deciding whether or not to read further.

There are many excellent online and printed guides that will take you step by step through the process of business planning in greater detail than I have space for here. See the Further Resources section at the end of the book.

Executive summary

Business description

Ownership and management

Strategic statement (50 words)

Marketing opportunities

Competitive advantages

Summary of financial projections

Section nine: Executive summary

The executive summary may be the only page that an external advisor or investor will read. Give it the BOOM! factor.

A BOOM!ING FUTURE

Reading *BOOM!* is just the beginning. What is important now is how you use the information within this book to reinforce the foundations of your business and your life in a focused and positive way.

Hopefully you now understand why discipline is so important in business. You need to ensure that everything you have been reminded of within these pages becomes fixed in routine and becomes a practical habit. The 7 Business Disciplines will help you stay on track when the going gets tough and must become an intrinsic part of the way you think, the way you act, the way you lead and the way you conduct your business.

In the current marketplace, every entrepreneur needs to develop the BOOM! factor in order to stand out from the crowd. It is not enough to simply aspire to be a BOOM!preneur – you need to become one. Success is not just about having a dream – it is about taking practical steps to achieve your goals and ambitions. Combine the practical elements of the 7 disciplines with passion, the right attitude and personal honesty.

- **Build** – develop your business responsibly with the future in mind
- **Own** – take personal ownership of your business decisions and outcomes
- **Operate** – in a professional, efficient and consistent way
- **Maintain** – create impact by maintaining your passion, enthusiasm and personal motivation. Where you lead others will follow.

My intention has been to inspire others to succeed and I hope that *BOOM!* delivers success to you. My wish is that you will benefit from the results as they impact on your business and your life. Remember, the difference between mediocrity and excellence is maintaining a passion for what you do.

BE PASSIONATE

Passionate about what you do

Passionate about why you are doing it

Passionate about being the best and willing to learn

Passionate about working hard

Passionate about your business

Passionate about making money

Passionate about people

Passionate about customer service

Passionate about finding solutions

Passionate about being successful

Passionate about life

Further Reading

Many successful business owners have taken inspiration and guidance from a handful of favourite and well-thumbed business books. The following mini-library includes a few favourites that I hope will help you on your path to business success.

The Beermat Entrepreneur: Turn your good idea into a great business (Mike Southon and Chris West) Pearson, 2002, 2009
     An excellent overview of the phases of growth that a business will go through in order to expand and achieve success.

The Definitive Business Plan: The fast-track to intelligent business planning for executives and entrepreneurs, 2nd edn (Richard Stutely) Prentice Hall/Financial Times, 2006

The Definitive Guide to Business Finance: What smart managers do with the numbers, 2nd edn (Richard Stutely) Prentice Hall/Financial Times, 2006
     Both of these guides by Richard Stutely will give you fine-grade detail on the planning and finance required for effective business management – but you will need an accountant to advise you too.

It's Not How Good You Are, It's How Good You Want To Be (Paul Arden) Phaidon, 2003
     Quite simply, brilliant. A must for every creative and original thinker.

Purple Cow: Transform your business by being remarkable (Seth Godin) Penguin, 2003
     An inspirational reminder of the need to strive to be extraordinary by the international marketing guru.

The Seven Habits of Highly Successful People: Powerful lessons in personal change (Stephen R. Covey) Simon & Schuster, 1989, 2004
     Covey explains the empowering impact of the principles of integrity, fairness, honesty and human dignity in life and business.

186

Smarter Business Start-Ups: Start your dream business
(Jon Smith) *52 Brilliant Ideas* series, Infinite Ideas Ltd, 2004
  Useful tips and ideas for all start-ups.

Start Your Own Business 2009: The ultimate step-by-step guide
(Ian Whiteling, editor) Crimson, 2009
  A comprehensive handbook of business management aimed at
small- and medium-sized enterprises.

The Tipping Point: How little things can make a big difference
(Malcolm Gladwell) Abacus, 2000
  The international bestseller about recognising moments of change.

The 22 Immutable Laws of Marketing (Al Reis and Jack Trout) Profile,
1993
  A short nugget of a book, written by two of the world's most
successful marketing strategists, it is full of real-life marketing stories
and anecdotes.

Further Resources

British Chambers of Commerce (BCC)
www.britishchambers.org.uk
There is a Chamber of Commerce in every county in Britain. Providing
support and advice on everything from employment law to trading
standards, the BCC is a bridge between local businesses and local
government. The website offers information for business start-ups.

Business Link
www.businesslink.gov.uk
Helpline: 08456 009 006
Business Link is a sound source of free advice for everyone in
business. Their website provides guidelines and up-to-date information
on everything from compiling a Business Plan to business growth, raising
finance, hiring or staff dismissal, VAT and tax returns.

Companies House

www.companieshouse.gov.uk

Contact centre: 0303 1234 500

Companies House has three main functions: to incorporate and dissolve limited companies; to examine and store company information that has been submitted in line with the Companies Act and related legislation; to make the information available.

Health and Safety Executive

www.hse.gov.uk

Ask an expert: 08453 450 055

The HSE protects people's health and safety by ensuring risks in the changing workplace are properly controlled. The organisation offers advice to businesses and individuals.

HM Revenue and Customs

www.hmrc.gov.uk

The main function of HMRC is to ensure that the correct amount of tax is paid at the right time. Although many people are daunted by the idea of contacting HMRC, their advisors are very helpful. The website offers a range of contact details depending on the nature and type of enquiry.

Institute of Directors

www.iod.com

Enquiries: 020 7766 8866

Most industries have a business club or organisation that provides a useful forum for networking, meetings and research. The IoD's network of locations extends across most major cities in the UK.

Intellectual Property Office

www.ipo.gov.uk

Enquiries: 08459 500 505

The IPO is responsible for advising on and granting intellectual property rights in the UK. They are your starting point for information relating to Patents, Trademarks, Design and Copyright.

Where to find an accountant

The best way to find an accountant is via word of mouth. However, the following associations can provide details of accountants in your area:

■ The Association of Chartered Certified Accountants (ACCA)

www.accaglobal.com

■ Chartered Institute of Management Accountants (CIMA)

www.cimaglobal.com

■ The Institute of Chartered Accountants in England and Wales (ICAEW)

www.icaewfirms.co.uk

■ The Institute of Chartered Accountants of Scotland (ICAS)

www.icas.org.uk

■ The Institute of Chartered Accountants in Ireland (ICAI)

www.icai.ie

See also: www.accountancyage.com/resources/top50

Where to find a solicitor

■ The Law Society of England and Wales

www.lawsociety.org.uk

■ The Law Society of Scotland

www.lawscot.org.uk

Where to find guidance on Employment law

■ The Chartered Institute of Personnel and Development (CIPD)

www.cipd.co.uk

■ Directgov

www.direct.gov.uk

Acknowledgements

Every successful venture begins with a great idea. That idea might be the result of one person's moment of inspiration or it may culminate from a lifetime of experience; but one thing is certain, no project can be completed without the support of friends or family and the help of a team of people willing and able to share the vision and make it happen.

During my time as owner and director of **Diva Cosmetics**, I recruited, trained and worked alongside the best team I could ever have wished for. They were there while I was learning many of the lessons described in this book – and I thank them for all they gave of themselves and for the fun, tears and laughter that we shared.

My accountant **Andrew Perriam** and my solicitor **Mark J. Clarke** have been my business confidants and advisors since the day Diva started and remain an essential part of my business ventures. Andrew's strategic ability is extraordinary. If only more accountants were like him. Mark's wisdom, patience and precision have safeguarded my business interests and been a life-saver on occasion. Thank you Andrew, thank you Mark, you've been there for me every step of the way.

More recently, as director of EMpwr, I am immensely grateful for the friendship and guidance of my exceptional PR consultant **Sue Blake** of Sue Blake Media. Her passion for excellence and 'purple cow' thinking matches my own. Sue has shown a unique ability to understand my vision and make it happen. The title BOOM! was her great idea.

I knew I had a story to tell, but I needed others to help me tell it. I'd like to thank **Sarah Sutton** for her writing skills; **Jenny Ng**, **Dawn Bates** and **Trish Burgess** for their astute editing; **Annette Peppis** for her wonderful page design; and **Sally Seward** for helping me to find a clear voice in the early days of EMpwr. They listened, captured and interpreted all I had to say. **Roger Hall** safeguarded book production. Thank you too to **Jennifer Drayton** of jennydmakeup.co.uk and to **Anthony Wood**, www.anthonywood.co.uk for a fabulous photoshoot.

My clients too have made a major contribution to this book. They not only consulted me about how to transform their businesses, but have been generous with their praise. In truth, I have learned as much from them about being a successful mentor as they have from me about being successful business owners.

At the heart of EMpwr is a sparkling creature called 'EM'. She appeared as if by magic from the creative mind of **Neil Stevens** of deshok.com. Neil has since created my website.

Most importantly, I'd like to thank **my husband Mark**, for his unswerving belief in me and all I want to achieve – for encouraging me to pursue my business plans while we raise our young family; for forgiving me when he is left juggling the children single-handed; and for listening to me and supporting me, no matter what.

And last, but definitely not least – **William, Charlie and Hattie** – I would like to thank you for being the best children your loving mummy could ever hope for.

Meet the contributors

The list following includes those who have kindly contributed to this book and features a selection of those I have worked with professionally and as a mentor.

Rachel Beresford was previously Office Accounts Manager at Diva Cosmetics.
"There were tears and laughter in working for Emma but hard work was always well rewarded and she earned our respect. Working with her was a great experience."

Mark J. Clarke LLB, Managing Partner, Clarke & Co Solicitors
A solicitor with nineteen years' experience in Employment Law, Mark started Clarke & Company in 1996. The firm specialises in Commercial Litigation, Employment Law and Personal Injury Work.
"Emma has energy, focus, passion and she knows what she wants. One of her core business strengths is in knowing when to ask for professional advice to help achieve her goals."

Nicky Connors joined Diva Cosmetics as Marketing Assistant on the day the company started and became Director of Product Development.
"Emma is an inspiration and I have learnt some of my most valuable lessons through her. Any business using Emma's disciplines

cannot fail to be a vibrant and successful one. This lady just doesn't do failure or compromise."

Barbara Cox, CEO, Nutrichef Ltd www.nutrichef.co.uk
Barbara became interested in healthy eating while living in Japan and went on to train as a nutritionist. Barbara founded Nutrichef in 2004. The team produces healthy meals and delivers them to people's homes. Barbara has been named Entrepreneur of the Year two years running.
"I knew immediately that Emma would be my ideal business mentor: she's been there, she's done it, her track record of accomplishments is fantastic; she was the perfect choice."

Sarah Isaacs, Owner, Kiteleys Solicitors Ltd www.kiteleys.co.uk
Sarah is an experienced litigator and was admitted as a Fellow of the Association of Law Costs Draftsman in 2004. Her company has been providing legal advice, specialising in personal injury, since 1992. Sarah took over as owner–manager in 2007.
"Emma is highly disciplined and focused; and that is what you need in a business mentor. Fortunately a lot of her energy and motivation also seem to rub off. Many of her tips and techniques are now being applied in my personal life as well as in my business life."

Andrew Perriam, Partner, Rothmans Chartered Accountants
www.rothmansllp.com
Andrew is a qualified Chartered Accountant and Corporate Finance Practitioner. His corporate clients range from listed companies to SMEs and charities. He provides advice on a broad range of areas ranging from accounts and taxation to general business guidance.
"When Emma decided to go into business on her own, I stuck with her. What you want from a client is lots of communication and plenty of business savvy, and Emma's very good at both."

Saskia Lankshear joined Diva as a new Product Development Coordinator and became Senior Account Manager.
"Emma set the bar very high and she could sometimes be a little intimidating to work for – but what successful business person isn't?

192

She motivated me to work hard and produce results and was the ideal business mentor."

Peter Read BSc (Econ.) ACII, Owner, Read Insurance Brokers Ltd

www.readinsurance.co.uk

Peter qualified as an Associate of the Chartered Insurance Institute in 1987 and now owns and manages Read Insurance Brokers Limited. He manages the insurance programmes for major companies both in the UK and overseas.

"What distinguishes Emma from other mentors is the sense that she is an integral part of my business and incredibly encouraging. She's so fired up and positive, she is a breath of fresh air."

George Whitmarsh, MBE, Managing Director, Global Integrity Ltd

www.global-integrity.uk.com

George had a distinguished career in the Royal Marines and Special Forces before setting up his business. His company specialises in risk mitigation and security management around the globe. George incorporates the principles that he learned during his military career to provide a quality service to his clients.

"Emma is my business conscience. If I find myself procrastinating an image of her pops up in my mind and she's saying, 'What have you achieved since our last meeting?' and then, 'What do you mean you've done nothing?' So I get on and get it done!"

Kate Woolston joined as a general assistant on the freight desk at Diva Cosmetics and was promoted to Accounts Manager a year later.

"Emma is the epitome of a 'can-do' attitude. There will never be an insurmountable obstacle; everything is possible. You could tell me anything that Emma was planning to do, no matter how ambitious and I would be 100 per cent confident that she would achieve it. I am still using her principles of business today, running our own business."

Index